THE
VANISHING
MAP

THE VANISHING MAP

A JOURNEY FROM LA TO TOKYO TO THE HEART OF EUROPE

STEPHEN BARBER

Oxford • New York

English edition
First published in 2006 by
Berg

Editorial offices:
First Floor, Angel Court, 81 St Clements Street, Oxford OX4 1AW, UK
175 Fifth Avenue, New York, NY 10010, USA

Berg is the imprint of Oxford International Publishers Ltd.

Library of Congress Cataloging-in-Publication Data
Barber, Stephen, 1961-
    The vanishing map / Stephen Barber.
        p. cm.
    Includes bibliographical references.
    ISBN-13: 978-1-84520-510-2 (hardback)
    ISBN-10: 1-84520-510-3 (hardback)
  1. Barber, Stephen, 1961—Travel. 2. Cities and towns. 3. Sociology,
Urban. I. Title.

    G465.B37 2006
    910.4—dc22

                                                                    2006014742

British Library Cataloguing-in-Publication Data
A catalogue record for this book is available from the British Library.

ISBN-13   978 1 84520 510 2 (Cloth)
ISBN-10   1 84520 510 3 (Cloth)

Typeset by JS Typesetting Ltd, Porthcawl, Mid Glamorgan.
Printed in the United Kingdom by Biddles Ltd, King's Lynn.

www.bergpublishers.com

Contents

Part I

City of Angels, City of Devils

1

By the time I reached the strange coastal city of Los Angeles, the dark continent of Europe had vanished from my mind.

All the way across the continent of America – named after a European: Amerigo Vespucci, whose face is represented on the altarpiece of the Ognissanti church in Florence – the airplane on autopilot had crossed vast terrains of iced land in darkness. The entire continent appeared frozen, from the Atlantic coast as far as the Sierra Nevada. That crust of ice locked the continent down as a black and gilt screen over which the shadow of the airplane passed, like a shimmering film image from the first moments of the history of cinema. Almost every zone of land was deserted, as though the continent of America was one of those yet to be discovered: all that was visible above the ice level were the raw peaks of mountain ranges, the serrated lips of volcanic craters and the obstinate curls of oxbow lakes, more deeply frozen still than the rest of the land. Every hour or so, viewed from the window of the airplane with its minuscule overhead light, an isolated community of human beings marked its presence so tenuously that its trace could, after a first glance to establish its ethnographic value, be wiped away without compunction: a few headlights of cars advancing erratically along the ice-stricken roads, and the scattered lights of town centers isolated from the nodal points of civilization, from which television images were being transmitted of terminal ice storms and of eggs fried on ice upon the pavements of urban America.

That planet below the airplane had a remarkable history, as far as its population was concerned. It was at some point around eleven millennia ago that the human species had begun to take the upper hand on that planet. Before that, it was a species of no account: always on the run and subject to sudden slaughter by larger creatures, and confined to inhabiting caves where the only occupation was the compulsive incision in rock of drawings of vulvas and screams. That species developed sexual concerns, then began a program of erasure which saw the eradication of most of its competitors for power over the planet. Gradually, it became preoccupied with ideas of religion, with revolution and colonial expansion, though those preoccupations invariably resulted in large-scale massacres and a condition experienced as one of futility. At this point, America was created. Towards the end of its moment of dominance, that human species even devised a means of technology by which one specimen could communicate with another over long distances, by means of an elegant block of plastic and metal that transmitted urgent sounds made by the tongue; there was even, at one point, the idea of a digital culture of metropolitan image-screens that would be the salvation of the planet's benighted population. But that species was always pre-eminently intent upon the devastation of the planet it inhabited, in order to render it ultimately void; its inhabitants began to dream more and more of leaving the planet, as had once occurred with the shooting of a spaceship – packed with human beings – to the planet's barren moon and back again.

Once the airplane had crossed the Sierra Nevada, the ice zone abruptly ended and the desert began: even in the darkness, the excoriated surface of the continent signaled a rip in the screen of America, and a plummet into another space of vision, between the mountains and the ocean. That annex to the continent was still burning. It seemed that even the maximal planetary heat of the desert failed to match the source of that incineration. And then the great apparition of Los Angeles started to conjure itself out of the night, endlessly: vast random networks of gasoline-propelled frenzy, studded with darkness and discharges of negation: regulated psychosis on an immense scale. The city was layered deep in images and oblivion, from the moment of its origin. Almost as soon as it had been colonized, that city had started to project its overriding obsessions with wealth and sex and exile – and the process of transmitting them through the medium of film, from the beginning of the twentieth century, had magnified those obsessions virulently, to a planetary scale. The surface of the city far below formed the residue of all of those images, stretched to their final articulation, as a crisscrossed, scarred pattern of skin and light, semen and pain, and ready to ignite again at any moment. The airplane from Europe started to come down, circling over the ocean and then accelerating towards the ground. When it had taken off, ten hours earlier, some emanation of Europe had remained clinging to its fuselage, like a desperate stowaway packed with a reserve of nostalgia; but the ice of America had gradually dissolved that aberrant presence, and by the time the airplane hit the runway, the last of that memory of Europe had evanesced in a white-heat backblast.

In the train from the airport, heading towards Watts, nervous Mexican boys carrying rods from their day of fishing on Redondo Beach sat among the South Central gangs, and the train passed freeways that ascended into the air to entangle themselves with other freeway complexes; the stations on the line culled their names from the numbers of those freeways and their intersections. Close to the station in Watts where the trains shifted direction, the forms of the Rodia Towers – alongside the railway tracks but located at the acute peripheries of vision – imprinted themselves in a veering sweep over the impending hallucination of the great corporate towers at the city's awry core; then, the city engulfs the eye.

5

2

At the far western edge of the continent of America, nothing could be further from Europe: the ocean stretches away to Cape Inubozaki at the eastern extremity of Japan, where a lighthouse surrounded by ramen fast-food stalls marks the point from which a succession of seaweed-encrusted rocks trails Japan away into extinguishment in the Pacific ocean. At Zuma Beach and Cape Inubozaki, the atmosphere is identical: groups of young surfers in black wetsuits wait patiently in the erratic surf for their moment of exhilaration, and the roaring air appears deoxygenated, as though anticipating the moment when a vast tectonic shift will violently concertina those two points together, the Juan de Fuca Plate buckling against the Philippine Plate like a train wreck, soldering the body of America to the body of Japan, to create an aberrant new world.

On the bus from Los Angeles Union Station to Zuma Beach, the shaven-headed driver talks benignly to a passenger about recent shootings of mutual friends as we head down Venice Boulevard, stopping at every fast-food outlet; several of the other passengers have their life's entire possessions with them, covering three or four seats, and disembarking with their multiple bags forms a complex operation, as though they were arriving for a lengthy convalescence at a central European spa town. The vast warehouse hoardings in Korean characters pass by, their declarations covering other inscriptions imprinted over the decades in indelible tea-paint on fire-blackened brick. Other passengers are in a glossolaliac state of excitation, mumbling to themselves about the coming apocalypse; two withdrawn cultists strike up an unexpected rapport when they recognize a shared vocal delirium, and pleasurably confirm one other's assertions on the imminent arrival of the Antichrist and on the devastating global event which has already taken place, and in whose invisible ruins this city now resides. But as the bus nears Santa Monica, that apocalyptic bliss palls, and the cultists gradually melt away, now exhausted and silent once again; by the time the ocean comes into view, only a scattering of wary Mexican day-workers remains, heading for manual work on wealthy estates in the hills above Malibu. Inland from the Pacific Coast Highway, the mountains appear sheared off by layers of warm mist, but the air above the ocean is infinitely transparent. It seems as though the bus could continue traveling indefinitely, swallowed by that intoxicating light, but the journey abruptly expires at Trancas Canyon, where an outpost of beachside shacks and a Starbucks coffee shop signal the end of the hallucinatory space of Los Angeles.

The surfers remained immobile in the ocean, all the way southwards to Point Dume: the retreating ocean was near-becalmed in a profound silence, tipped over the edge of the world at slow-motion velocity, as though that shoreline marked a paper cut sharply incised into all mapped space, beyond which the fissured city and the seismic ocean peeled away from one another, each plunging into autonomous free fall. For the nineteenth-century European explorers of California, driven from the famine lands of Sweden and Ireland, that terminal point of the American continent formed a paradisiacal boundary, filigreed with gold, which needed to be aimed for with brutal determination, even when their trajectories westwards through the furnace canyons of Death Valley led them to murderous dead-ends. And the central European entrepreneurs exiled from Hungary and Poland, who transplanted the American film industry from New York to California in the second decade of the twentieth century, concocted identical visions of ecstatic void space from the raw sensory material of exile and lust. The obsessions of Europe had seized hold of that iridescent zone, but only the most tenaciously conjured sensations ever took tangible form at that vanishing point of America.

In the darkness, I took the final bus back from Trancas Canyon into the city, now accompanied by the most obdurate of the surfers, who had waited until the last instant to abandon their desire for momentary flight, and sat subdued and dripping over their surfboards. Then time shattered as the city closed in. By the time the bus finally reached Main Street at midnight, the derelict thousands-strong population of downtown Los Angeles had already submerged itself under cardboard containers on the pavements, beneath the empty facades and blown neon roof-signs of the avenue's once-grand, now-ruined hotels. Under the vast chandeliers of Union Station, the armchaired arrivals hall had emptied out too, every train gone for the night, with only the Las Vegas overnight coach revving outside on the tarmac.

3

You can move at will, taking your body and eyes with you, oscillating between the cinematic and the digital, in downtown Los Angeles: but the act of traversing the downtown grid of streets horizontally, block by block, propels you back and forward, through two spaces in a state of acute repulsion from one another. The north–south axis of Spring Street forms an urban boundary where the enveloping emanation of wealth from the sheer corporate towers of the western side of downtown evanesces suddenly; east from that border, the streets radiate their poverty as vast agglomerations of human flesh, transacting an extreme minimum of products with the maximal gestural and vocal exclamation. The great century-old hotels of Main Street visible from the late-night Zuma Beach bus, still majestic in their desolation in darkness, are stripped to the wracked bone in daylight, their crumbling foyers alternately absorbing and spouting a momentary clientele of the massed destitute. The thousands of homeless inhabitants of those avenues remain marooned in the city's merciless desert glare: leaning against walls, scuffling among one another for fast food and alcohol remnants, waiting. Threading through that crushed population, the frantic Mexican and El Salvadorian street-traders move at another speed, as though overlayered from a parallel universe upon that disintegrating, decelerating world.

All along the now-ravaged vertical avenue of Broadway, lavish cinema-palaces were constructed in the first decades of the twentieth century, with intricately stone-carved Moorish facades, gilded travertine-marble foyers and extravagant marquees erected to announce their alluring names: the Million Dollar Theater, the Los Angeles Theater, the Orpheum Theater. Films for gala premieres could be rushed across the city straight from the editing tables of Hollywood, their splices still hot from the cutter's hands, to be activated into compulsive images within those incendiary sites. But cinema in Los Angeles collapsed long before the digital image's arrival: the space of the downtown was arbitrarily divided, razored like celluloid, and the cinemas found themselves on the accursed side. By the end of the 1970s, they had already shown all the hard-core pornography that the eyes of Los Angeles could work to absorb, and had lapsed into neglect. I abandoned my horizontal crossings of the downtown to explore every facade and foyer, from the Bradbury Building junction down to the avenue's southern end; some of the auditoria were barricaded shut, others still penetrable, guarded by creased-faced old men. A few cinema auditoria had been gutted entirely, then converted into cacophonic clothes-markets; the neon letters – each the size of human bodies – that formed their names had gradually come unstuck, crumbling to the pavement below, until those names had vanished into the city, leaving behind the anonymous vagrants of cinema. Other film-palaces had become the domain of religious cultists, and for a few moments at a time I embraced imminent apocalypses or messianic arrivals to enter those illuminated spaces, where the still-standing empty screens above the congregations sonically projected delirious prayers and lamentations. Film had been erased from the city at its core.

The last film image viewed in the heart of Los Angeles would have been the convulsing face of a mustachioed late-1970s pornography star, spurting over the stained screen before a blasé, near-vacated cinema audience. And once that image had burned out into the air, leaving the moribund cinema's dust-encrusted amplifiers reverberating with a terminal orgasm, the city had been left with the work of envisioning its own images: imagining the transformation of that immense urban coagulation of human bodies and sensory uproar into some kind of first image of life. But no image had yet been made.

By the time I reached the base of Broadway and the final annulled cinema, the light was fading out over the city, to be replaced by the illumination of the corporate towers on the far side of that division in the city's space. Many of those towers' facades succinctly announced only the name of their affiliation: Deutsche Bank, Sony Corporation; pierced in the faces of others, high-definition image-screens transmitted short digital animations lauding their occupants' financial power. Those towers encompassed the low-lying forms of art museums, as though concerned to shield them from the fate of those abject cinemas, three or four avenues away to the east; but at night, with all but the most devoted of its commuting occupants departed for the endless suburbs, that acetylene terrain appeared to hold no power at all. The nodal point between those towers formed a plateau high above the city, the California Plaza, pitted by an artificial lake and a deserted concert arena; but almost the entire city was blocked from view by the surrounding towers, irresistibly focusing the eye towards those desolate avenues to the east, silent and decontaminated from this level.

Over the city, the sky was cleansed too with its night's re-mission from gasoline build-up; helicopters with searchlights were tracking stolen cars far beyond the downtown avenues, and every few minutes, a jet appeared over the summit of the Deutsche Bank tower, rising above the dark wall of the San Bernardo Mountains, heading non-stop to Europe or to the frozen zones between.

4

America enjoys its wars: those wars created it, in originatory skirmishes which left only handfuls of dead but brought into being apparitions such as the space of California; but when those conflicts were eventually transposed beyond the secure ground of America, they veered out of control, with slaughtered bodies amassed together on the beaches of Normandy and the jungle tracks of Vietnam. America's own boundaries became ever more corroded, those edges gaping and stuffed with vulnerable flesh, but still far too dispersed and stretched for the successful prosecution of incursive border wars. Even the last-ditch defenders of Japan, in 1945, had to renounce their retaliatory project of all-out human-torpedo assaults on the

American coasts, in the face of that vast, protective dispersal. Every enemy of America, from Hitler on, dreamed of the aerial technology necessary for realizing the sudden, concentrated destruction of New York City, but Los Angeles remained too fluidly shrouded in its own dissolution ever to be envisaged for attack. It cannot be destroyed.

Instead, California seeps. On the tramway that runs from the waterfront corporate towers of San Diego to the Mexican border city of Tijuana – by legend, the most crossed frontier on the planet – the passengers transit worlds in a dense vocal cacophony, crushed together and sweating anxiety. As the tram traverses the southern suburbs of San Diego, past the naval dockyards, more and more passengers attempt to board; that crush abruptly flickers over to Europe in my watching eyes, to the photographs by Boris Mikhailov of the overflowing trams of the still-Soviet city of Kharkov, already loaded far beyond their corporeal capacity but with gaps forcibly jarred open by sheer desperation, and to the early-1990s night trams of the Marzahn suburb of eastern Berlin, alcohol-fueled battlegrounds in motion for bloody confrontations between neo-Nazi and anarchist factions. But here, as the tram passes Chula Vista and the mountains of northern Mexico begin to appear in the distance, the atmosphere remains benign. Everything is still new and fresh, on this border in heaving movement, however engrained and ancient the broken gravity of the faces of returning Mexican day-workers appears. Only the thin covering of a century or two of provisional subjugation lies over this terrain, alongside the profound accumulation of oppression and massacre layered through millennia into every last corner of Europe. Everything here is still under construction.

Some of the American tourists on the tram grow exasperated at the crush, and abandon the journey halfway through the hour-long stretch from San Diego, standing on the platforms of stations in half-built industrial estates to smoke cigarettes and wait for the next tram, which will be even fuller. They are from the cities of America, each with an ongoing story to tell about familial calamity whose narration is only ever momentarily suspended. The tram is moving on, leaving them behind. When the city finally appears, across the Tijuana River, sprawling in tightly gridded cubes of housing on a sheer hillside, under thin black twists of rain, all tension in the tram evaporates. It seems now that everyone will be crossing that border, and reaching that city. I stand at the frontier point for an hour and watch the pulses of bodies in either direction. They have a compulsive desire to exit one space and emerge on the other side. But on the American side of the border, in the tenuous zonal space of San Ysidro, the traces of human civilization to be reached by those crossing figures are desultory: a few fast-food outlets, shuttered offices promising loans and money-transfers, and shacks for low-grade prostitution and alcohol. Those who arrive in America must wonder what strange and uninhabitable country they have happened upon. Even on infrared satellite photographs of the American side of the border, digitally enhanced to the maximal degree by optical scanning, nothing is discernible to the eye there; so you cannot stop, you must go on.

The sleek train back to Los Angeles from San Diego follows the coast: the sun is going down over the ocean and by the time we reach Los Angeles, it will be dark, and the downtown towers will be illuminated, clustered together in isolation above the scarified, lethal face of the city. In the seats in front of me and behind me, the few passengers are talking on cellphones, arranging parties, bemoaning illnesses, oblivious to it all.

5

Far into the night, in the drinking bars and karaoke clubs of Little Tokyo, stranded between the city's burning downtown towers and its meltdown avenues of dereliction, that consuming oblivion is pursued with wholehearted tenacity. Los Angeles envelops the space of Little Tokyo, but it is also a world away; the drunken tofu salesmen from Osaka, the fashionably holidaying girls from Tokyo's Harajuku or Shibuya shopping avenues, and the now-entrenched fifth-generation Japanese escapees, all remain meshed together within the same boundary-space, which provides a momentary capsule of exemption from the hallucination of Los Angeles. The windows of the street-level bars are smeared and dripping with alcoholic perspiration. But unlike the night alleyways of Tokyo's Shinjuku district of all-night full-on bars and sex hotels, the Kabukicho, the inhabitants of this sanctuary can never reel out onto the streets, accompanied by thousands of similarly incapacitated celebrants; the Los Angeles avenues outside form severe and forbidding channels, studded with monuments and museums marking both the mass incarceration of Los Angeles' Japanese residents during the 1940s Pacific War, and the bravery of the city's Japanese-émigré soldiers in defeating their former countrymen in that war. In the center of Little Tokyo's main avenue, a monument-slab of mourning to the astronaut of Japanese origin, Ellison S. Onizuka – whose Challenger rocket blasted itself apart above the skies of America, ignited by a mix of liquid hydrogen and liquid oxygen fuels, before billions of watching eyes on live television – adds another contrary form to those fragments of memory, aberrant presences in the night space of Los Angeles.

Through the night for weeks on end, then months, I crossed the surfaces of Los Angeles, on foot, from Little Tokyo to the end of Broadway, from the corporate towers on Bunker Hill to Union Station, or rode as a passenger along the splintered, sensorial avenues of Hollywood, through Watts and Little Armenia, and out northwards to the raw ocher canyons of Valencia and Acton. The nocturnal air kept pouring in through the windows of the car, from the toxic furor of Sunset Boulevard to the chilled heat of the Mojave Desert's deep silence. In Los Angeles, it seemed as though, always glancing at the surface and always distracted to the far perimeter of America, I was still heading into the oblivious heart of America. And, whenever it became dawn and the lights of the downtown towers were finally extinguished for the night, then I started thinking about Europe: if the cities of Europe had somehow resisted the self-erasure that annulled America, and still held the memory of their calamities and transformations, of their upheavals and ecstasies, then that memory had to be located at the very heart of Europe, deep in its dead center, in one image or one body that engulfed and contained the infinity of all of those memories of Europe. And so I finally decided to try and find that memory.

On the way to the airport, for the flight out of Los Angeles, I took a detour and left the 110 Freeway to see the Rodia Towers for once in daylight. Those lavishly pinnacled towers of debris – constructed over decades by an impoverished Italian laborer on his small plot of land, as a festive obsessional memory of his homeland, armatured like the skeleton of an emaciated human body, then abandoned by him without a second thought on their completion – had survived the Watts riots of 1965 and the earthquake of 1994. Now they stood gated behind a high wire fence, its facade placarded with institutional praise for the governor of California. A few children from the area's minuscule wooden houses were milling around the fence and the concrete plaza alongside the towers. They approached me to say: "People around here are crazy." My driver laughed and waved the children away. The behavior of the population of Los Angeles will remain a mystery until the end of time.

It was still light as the airplane took off for Europe, but looking down, I soon lost all sense of the endless grids of avenues. The spikes of the downtown towers appeared to have vanished, or to have been moved to another part of the city; even the ocean seemed as though its place had been inversed. The entire city was spinning and disintegrating as the plane made turns, gaining height. All of my careful mental assembling of the space of the city, compiled on innumerable walks and journeys across its expanse, abruptly scrambled and fell in upon itself. Then the airplane roared across the San Bernardo Mountains and that vision of the city was gone forever.

Part II

The Heart of Europe

6

Flying over Europe, there's nothing below: Europe is absent at ground level, living or surviving only in the crushed layers of debris stretching far under its surface, in the air above its cities, in its images, and in the human bodies infinitely crossing and losing themselves over its expanse.

The decrepit airplane hit turbulence storms as soon as it reached the heart of Europe, as though it were entering a vortex as it moved deeper into that engulfing space. The few passengers were spread out, but I could hear curses and prayers in Czech and Albanian as the rattling airplane convulsed in the seismic air. Through a break in the black clouds, I suddenly saw the southeastern suburbs of Prague: the vast swathes of concrete apartment towers stretching out like flailing arms from the city, their windows still illuminated at midnight with the indigo glow of television screens, then the tight conglomeration of shoddy business towers at the lower edge of the old city. We veered crazily into descent over the Vltava River and the Karlův Most bridge, the view of the city cut and flickering like a near-disintegrated film, between banks of cloud and torrents of ice. The airplane accelerated for the runway at Ruzyně Airport, but the airport itself was invisible under a ferocious ice storm heading from the west and driving near-horizontally at a raw velocity over the ground, pounding the left side of the airplane; abruptly, a few hundred meters from the runway, the airplane lifted itself into a tenuous floating position, its engines in overdrive, as though suspended within that storm and prepared to remain that way indefinitely, pinioned by ice above the earth's surface. Inside the fuselage, the curses and prayers had turned to silence. Then the airplane gradually gained height, zigzagging through the torn air until the oblivious city was visible once again.

Once we were above the worst storm-level, the pilot narrated the crisis in Czech, Albanian and finally in broken English: we would keep circling the city for a time, in the hope that the storm would clear; then, when fuel became short, we would have to make for another airport. And so we began to circle, and I watched out for sites by which to cohere my eyes, between the raging pulses of ice: again and again, as the airplane slowly looped, going nowhere, I picked out the coagulated suburban nodes of the Modřany apartment blocks, the soaring tower of the Hotel International with its red-starred summit, the Letná Plain's empty plinth where the world's largest monument had once stood, and the vast mausoleum on the Žižkov Hill; on other circuits, I saw nothing at all, blinded by the storm. After an hour or so, the pilot gave up and headed east without announcing a new destination, and we began to fly at low altitude over great tracts of quarried forests and provincial settlements bordered by sprawling industrial zones, their gangs of night-shift workers burrowing into the ground, lit up by acetylene flares on wooden poles. The passengers sat subdued, desolate, desperate; any insurrection was foreclosed in that battered can of stale air, careering lost over the now-featureless black ground below, as its engines ignited its last reserves of fuel. My only consolation was that I could feel the presence of Europe somewhere high up in the lacerated air we were traversing, as an exhilarating malediction with the power to annul whatever riled it. At a certain point, the pilot announced that we would attempt to land at Ostrava, at the far end of the country: every other airport in central Europe was closed to us.

On the tarmac at the tiny Ostrava Airport, with its neon-inscribed, corrugated-iron terminal building and rutted runway, the passengers grew unruly: some of them had been heading for Ostrava as their final destination anyway, and they pleaded to be let out of the airplane before the storm hit here too, but the pilot refused. Even the mascara'd, hard-bitten stewardesses wanted to leave the airplane, arguing with the pilot that it was better at all costs to hire a bus and drive the passengers back through the night, though they conceded at last that no highway existed between Ostrava and Prague, the journey would take at least twelve hours, and the roads would be blocked in any case. After an hour or two, a truck appeared out of the darkness to refuel the airplane; a lugubrious man threw bucketfuls of opaque liquid, with the consistency of semen, over the ice-clotted wings, then vanished again. Everything grew calm, and the passengers began to sleep. Then that same storm duly arrived out of the west, beating around the airplane for three or four hours and coating the runway in an impenetrable layer of solid ice. Finally, the pilot grew exasperated at the impasse and announced we were taking off again: Ruzyně Airport might reopen by the time we reached it. Before anyone could react, he wheeled the groaning airplane onto the runway's slithering crust and then took off perfectly from the glacial surface. At dawn, back over Prague, the city was gold and glowing, and the storm had gone.

7

Even back on the ground, I could still feel the compulsion of that same centrifugal force of indefinitely circling the city, which the passengers of the marooned airplane had been subjected to, their eyes attempting to catch guiding traces of the heart of Europe, on that journey through the frozen night: without the arbitrary cut-off point of its fuel gauge moving towards zero, the airplane could have continued its futile mission, propelled gradually deeper and in tighter circles as its passengers scanned the city below, until the wings finally broke apart, until those passengers lapsed into psychosis or delirium.

I started my own circling of the city from the Letná Plain, high up above the Vltava River. In the communist era, that plain had been transformed into a park, with a large space reserved for parades of the country's impassioned population – the only one in Europe to have voted for communism – in front of its leaders. All through the first half of the 1950s, an immense granite statue of Stalin was gradually constructed, at the edge of the plain that overlooked the city: the figure of Stalin was poised on the rim of that sheer precipice, accompanied by smaller statues of workers, peasants and soldiers. That statue, intended as an act of seduction for the capricious, aging Stalin, took so long to design and build that, by the time it was completed, he had already died. But it was still the largest monument in the world, visible from every point in the city. Photographs taken during the summer after its completion showed excited children in pioneer costumes entering the two great gateways into the vault below the statue; every evening at dusk, two huge brass urns at either side of the statue's plinth were filled with oil and ignited, so that the beneficent face of Stalin could be lit up by fire throughout the night. But soon after the statue was unveiled, Stalin had been denounced by his successor, and the population of Prague was instructed to erase his presence. In 1962, after standing above the city for only a few years, the statue was dynamited; but it had been so painstakingly constructed, to last for many centuries, that the first four attempts failed, only superficially scarring the surface of Stalin's face. Finally, the largest collection of premium-grade explosives ever assembled was drilled deep into every joint of the statue. Photographs of the resulting explosion showed a cataclysmic detonation, with infinite fragments of Stalin propelled in every direction; the noise of the explosion could be heard as far away as Dresden. Although the urns and plinth survived intact, nothing remained of the statue except for those pulverized splinters of granite.

I walked over the empty space, abandoned now for well over four decades and closed-off by tattered wire fencing, where the statue had stood. Apart from a scattering of skater-boys performing somersaults on the concrete expanses alongside the site, it was deserted. The raised, mosaic'd ground on which the statue had been constructed was left untouched, although it had warped under the explosion's impact and formed unusable terrain for the skater-boys who surrounded it; the pounded granite remnants lay interspersed with the amassed shards of broken beer bottles. Otherwise, no trace of that all-consuming aberration subsisted. But the vast urns alongside the statue's site still remained in pristine condition, their surfaces now coated in layered decades of graffiti, from the eroded, low-quality house-paint of the final phases of communism to the fluorescent spraycanned tags of the subsequent years. To the left of the statue's site, on the side of the now-extinguished urn that faced away from the city, someone had inscribed in black paint: "Hearth of Europe." I climbed up onto the plinth and looked inside the burnished interior of the urn; but it was empty, apart from a few rusted Coca-Cola cans and a discarded container for a Fuji DV cassette. Any surviving ashes of Europe's obsessions had been long-dissolved in the contaminated rain sweeping over from the city's industrial zones.

Below the urn, the bolted wooden gateway into the vault beneath the statue's site had been indented with a vertical line of holes, punched as though to allow whatever still lay inside to breathe. That entrance had also been barricaded with a protective framework of metal bars, in their turn covered with spraycanned paint in botched attempts to inscribe tags or denunciations onto the gateway's resistant surface: those efforts had instead formed inept images of wildly moving bodies, flailing or dancing. Through the holes, I could just make out the shapes of decrepit wooden chairs and tables, covered in decades of dust, but the gateway could no longer be prized open. I searched the entire facade of the monument for traces of its original inscriptions; all that remained was a horizontal succession of small stone tablets on the lower level of the plinth, their overwritten surfaces now corroded and damaged, but each one still legibly recording an exclaimed homage to Stalin from the population of each city of Czechoslovakia. No malediction or ecstasy, in the languages of Europe, can ever be entirely expunged.

8

And no city can be mapped except through the body. Each dawn, from that erased but seminal site on the Letná Plain, I began an impelled circuit of the city on foot, using its four principal railway stations as the nodal points of that journey. Outside the Bartolomějská Convent, confiscated and adapted by the secret police in the communist era for the incarceration and interrogation of dissidents, the long line of the homeless or poverty-stricken inhabitants of the old city had already formed before first light, with hours to wait until the nuns opened a hatch to cursorily hand to each of them their triangular chunk of rye bread and bowl of soup, which they gulped instantly, amassed there on the crooked pavement, chasing the hot liquid with swallows of pure spirit alcohol or dawn-chilled beer. Reaching that starting point on the Letná Plain already entailed a vision of a zone beyond time, that ricocheted endlessly, mutating from city to city right across eastern Europe, encompassing every group of huddled human figures fixed at stalls and tram stops and outlets of momentary mercy, at the points where any transformation in the face of the city could only create another free-falling collapse of time.

From the urn at Stalin's vanished feet, I headed northeast through districts of fissured apartment blocks and hissing factory chimneys to the Holešovice Station, now encased in a huge shopping complex, with the platforms forming an afterthought annex to the surrounding supermarkets and fast-food concessions. The night train from the northern European coast would arrive at arbitrary points in the early morning, the passengers stunned by exhaustion as they stumbled through the labyrinthine station hall, trying to find their way to street level. From Holešovice, I turned south over the Vltava River, crossing patches of derelict ground bordered by ornate buildings that remained poised in stasis, at a moment between incipient decrepitude and lush reconstruction, until I reached the Masarykovo Station, the first constructed in Prague, opened in 1845 as a terminus located close to the old core of the city and now reduced to forming the destination point of commuter trains from that city's northern peripheries. By mid-morning, the station had moved through its rush-hour crush and grown calm, with tiny coagulations of intent figures around the wooden stalls selling tenth-hand pornography magazines, and regular sweeping movements across its space performed by the station's permanent inhabitants, as they scanned the levels of vulnerability of its more transient occupants. Apart from the erection of a few half-hearted digital image-screens and hoardings, the station had been untouched since its construction, and gaps in the delicate iron roof threw down vertical bands of sunlight, indented with human shadows, onto the polished stone flooring. But to the southeast, at the Hlavni Station, any sense of calm was supplanted by a permanent uproar in that third station's lightless concourse, constructed in the 1970s in orange concrete and saturated with its feuding vagrant population, too enmeshed in their alcohol-propelled bad blood to do more than tenuously grab at the arms of the passengers traveling at maximal speed from the street outside to the platforms. But above that infernal ground level, the station's original concourse had somehow survived, inhabited by a few stray or lost figures, transplanted into a parallel universe that was accessed only via an unmarked, urine-soaked stairwell. Those bemused figures sat at café tables under the vast, arma- tured dome of that obsolete space, with its abandoned ticket booths and damp-peeling imperial insignia. Through the windows on one side of that original concourse, trucks and cars could be seen careering around the city's elevated ring road, and through the windows on the other side, trains revved and sizzled as they prepared for departure, across the plains of central Europe; but caught between those two channels, that slowly corroding space enforced its own silence and stillness. I sat for a moment under that near-forgotten, dust-filamented roof, its dome soaring vertically, presciently shaped like a Méliès space-rocket's cone, and now ready in its oblivion to wrench the entire city up from its fragile moorings and transport its population away to another, magical variant of Europe.

The final part of my circling of the city took me back across the Vltava to the Smíchovské Station, its concourse once again populated with glossolaliac vagrants, but now concertina'd so tightly into the narrow station hall that there was no option other than cohabitation between that derelict population and the waiting passengers, blown back by iced winds from the platforms overhead. As a result, the dense textures of human acts oscillated seamlessly between desperation and banality, under the concourse's vast Stalin-era mural of contented workers and peasants. But when the evening's last train for Mariánské Láznê was announced, the population abruptly halved, the derelicts gaining a luxurious monopoly until dawn over the terminally dirt-encrusted floors and benches, and I left too, circuiting the riverbank northwards until I arrived back on the Letná Plain, with the night city illuminated below me.

9

The night possesses its puncture points at the heart of Europe, into which memory surges with split-second aberrance, abruptly overturning the human body that carries that memory, and overturning too the contemporary city with its phosphorescent facades and animated digital image-screens. The night is a silencer of the caprices and brutalities that impel Europe, and a generator of apparitions, returned from the dead, that countermand and revivify its cities' boulevards and alleyways: whatever is returned from the dead, upon the cities of Europe, forms a presence that breaks the contemporary moment into brittle shards.

Each month or so in the strange moment of flux and chaos after the end of the communist era, I took the slow night train from Berlin to Vienna; the train would lose most of its irascible passengers at Dresden, then continue southwards, almost empty, along the river valleys of northwestern Czechoslovakia, suspending its journey in Prague for two hours at the Hlavni

Station, for no good reason, before continuing at four in the morning for the final dawn stretch to Vienna. I would leave the concretized orange concourse at speed, dodging between the previous generation of its alcoholic or disheartened inhabitants, through the park in front of the Hlavni Station, the pathways dense with its new contingent of Ukrainian teenaged prostitutes, and head into the old city, as far as I could go, pivoting round at the exact midpoint of that suspended interval of time, and returning to the station just as the engine unwillingly revved back into life for the journey's final leg. In those slices of the night, from two until four, in the first months of 1990, the city was inflicting a frenetic transformation upon itself. Almost every building appeared covered in scaffolding, held together at the last moment before collapse, the facades rubbed raw and cracked apart by acid pollution and neglect, showering dust and debris on the yelling, exhilarated street-population below. That icy night city already held the initial pulse of its sudden influx of young Americans, which would grow over the next year into an immense population, tens of thousands in strength, existing within an autonomous medium of drug- and alcohol-fueled lust that eventually left Prague behind, transplanting itself in predatory zigzags onto other cities, right across eastern Europe; its tangents became marked in semen and the steam from deliriously dancing bodies, from Tallinn to Constanța, amassing into a hallucinatory screen of wealth, pressed down gratuitously over crumbling and still-traumatized cities. That population's emanations of ecstasy gradually evanesced as it finally died away, leaving behind the imprinted memory traces of an awry succession of phantom sub-cities over the cities of Europe.

Sometimes, on the deserted Karlův Most bridge at three in the morning, looking down at the river, it felt then as though that surplus new population in gorgeous delirium had been created only to incite the vast populations of the city's dead to mark their own presence back upon that city: to wake the dead, amassed under and around the city in dense residual layers of invasions, massacres, feuds, suppressions, each propelled by its own urgent rationale or vision or will for power. But, heading back to the Hlavni Station through the crush of itinerant bodies – exiled uniquely by lust, into phantom space – it was clear that city had fallen oblivious to any confrontation with its histories and woundings, and that blissful fall was a deliverance.

10

To reach another memory of bliss in the city, backwards in time from that blasé, drug- and lust-fueled invasion of 1990, demanded a long, careering reverse-movement, within the adhesive domain of photographic or film images, back across fifty or sixty years of suppression and massacre, through photographs of the gasoline-scarred body of Jan Palach, who set fire to himself on the Václavské Náměstí square in 1969 in his refusal of the Soviet invasion of the previous year, back through the images of the detonation of Stalin's statue in 1962, on through film and photographs of the National Socialist occupation of the city, in scratched or blurred images of incinerated and hanged citizens in the wake of the 1942 assassination of Reinhard Heydrich, Hitler's protector of the subjugated city, ambushed and shot by partisans in its northern suburbs – with that movement across the time of images eventually bursting backwards through the boundary of Hitler's invasion of 1939. Finally, images of the city's bliss could be tracked down again in the short documentary films made between 1928 and the mid 1930s, by urban filmmakers who would be exiled or killed in the subsequent years. City films were being made throughout Europe in that period, reinventing or anatomizing cities, from Dziga Vertov's films of Moscow and Odessa to Walter Ruttmann's films of Berlin. In those films of Prague, the night city became an arena of exhilaration, traversed exploratively by its ecstasy-intent inhabitants, who moved between bars and clubs under facades of burning neon exclamations; by day, those same human figures still carried no constraints, and wandered at will, entranced, on foot and by tram, isolated and tracked by the film camera's eye, round from the city's heart to its suburban industrial-zones and back again. The films' titles carried that exhilaration and urban flux with precision: *Prague in the Glow of Light, We Live in Prague,* and Alexandr Hackenschmied's *An Aimless Walk.* After those few years of scanning the city's capriciously shifting life, the filmmakers themselves became subjected to a contrary, global uprootedness that cast them beyond Europe: Hackenschmied, who had worked on a film protesting the Sudetenland's annexation in 1938, fled to Paris in the following year, at the moment of Hitler's invasion of Prague, then moved on to Los Angeles – where, in collaboration with his wife Maya Deren, he made the film *Meshes of the Afternoon,* the seminal work of American underground cinema – and finally re-rooted himself in New York, compacting his name to Alexander Hammid in the process. At the same moment as those films had begun to be made, at the end of the 1920s, the sensorial radiance of the city's first independent decade, after the creation of the Czechoslovak Republic, was abruptly vanishing, with the onset of Europe-wide economic calamity and political extremity, and the film image-traces of Prague intimated a bliss that was already shot awry, experienced by human figures who circuit and cross the city in those images, in an endless elation that will be imminently, violently terminated. From that point on, the city detached itself from those film images, and escalated forwards again in time, impelled by invasive forces of slaughter or oppression, until that movement finally froze, in insurgence, fifty years on, for the city to be inhabited by that crazed, transient population of American children, in its 1990 incarnation.

Those film-city images of Prague from the 1920s and 1930s remained scattered, tenuous ones, but through them, a moment of urban bliss survived, embedded ineradicably against engulfing histories of atrocity.

11

On the seventh day of circling the city on foot, from railway station to station, that journey started to come apart, fraying off into aberrant excursions. As I headed back to the Letná Plain that afternoon, the sight of the white marble tower of the Hotel International over the edge of that circuit made me divert abruptly from my intended destination at the site of Stalin's statue, to head instead through the backstreets of the Dejvice district, until I stood in the plaza outside that vast hotel, whose prominent tower I had tracked from the stormbound airplane's window, a week earlier; I entered the chandelier'd lobby with its intricate friezes and mosaics of the peasants and workers' state, and took a room for the night.

Even in that city, which had applied the maximum explosive power to the work of detonating and erasing Stalin from its face, his presence still resurged, as though those gestures of erasure screened an ultimate attachment of some kind. And for my own journey, the act of cracking apart the obsessional circuit I had walked for seven days, away from the site of the statue on the Letná Plain, still irresistibly placed me back at a location in which Stalin remained the central determinant. That hotel had been built for the communist regime by the country's leading artisans in the early 1950s, during the same moment as the Letná Plain statue's construction, with limitless expense, displacing centuries-old houses to open out space for its surrounding parkland; the hotel's grandiose architecture exactly emulated that of the Palace of Culture and Sciences that had been personally gifted to the people of Warsaw by Stalin. Originally intended as a military officers' hospital in the western suburbs of the city, the building soon became a hotel fit for dignitaries and visiting communist leaders, with floor upon floor of gilt-fitted ballrooms and salons, tapering upwards to its red-starred summit. But by the early 1990s, the hotel had grown near-derelict as it passed from owner to oblivious owner; finally, an Austrian property conglomerate acquired it, in order to tap lucratively into the developing Europe-wide nostalgia for the obsolete monuments of communism, renaming it the "Hotel Stalin" and adopting for the soundtrack of its website the score to the Soviet director Michail Chiaureli's 1949 film *The Fall of Berlin*, in which Stalin triumphantly arrives by airplane in Berlin to congratulate the celebrating Soviet troops, only moments after they seize control of the Reichstag. Stalin's great-nephew, the Georgian neo-fascist politician Lavrentij Pavlovich Dzhugashvili, was then hired by the property conglomerate as the honorary hotel manager, in order to greet guests in an adept mixture of German and English, dressed in a white marshal's uniform adorned with modestly few medals, his facial features uncannily resembling those of his great-uncle, though lacking the pockmarked indentations of the original.

Even such strategies failed to attract an adequate clientele for the hotel, with its endless hundreds of luxurious rooms, ascending over many tiered stories connected by ornate staircases; the hotel then reacquired its initial name, Dzhugashvili returned to his hometown of Gori, and the website was redesigned with a soundtrack of sophisticated systems music. I explored the hotel's vertical space, through empty, lush red-carpeted corridors, and took the rattling elevator up to the top floor of immense suites; from that elevation, the city dipped and rose eastwards, buckled over its valleys. I wandered around the landscaped parkland at dusk, virtually the only guest in the entire hotel; it seemed as though Stalin had finally fallen out of favor and that totalitarian nostalgia was no longer a prized asset for the hotel's scarce clientele. The Armani-suited new manager told me that plans were now well underway for the building to be reinvented, against the historical grain, as a New York-style art deco hotel; although the red star on its summit was too pivotally fixed to the tower's structure to be removed, that tower would now be recast as a perverse variant of the Chrysler Building. But late that night, as every night in the heart of Europe, with the sound of the final trams grinding to a halt in the plaza outside the hotel, I caught the silent television transmitting a documentary about the acts of Stalin, the images almost lost between those of the engulfing pornography channels, but obstinately holding on.

12

I checked out of the Hotel International and continued my circuit of the city, as though that night had formed an apparition only momentarily able to divert the indefinite momentum of circling over and through the city's layers. One afternoon, on the stretch between the Holešovice and Masarykovo Stations, in a blizzard of ice, I lost my way, blocked by a cacophony of building work along the roads between factory zones, beside the area where overhead train tracks densely converged and split apart, east of the Florenc district. In that nameless site, the nineteenth-century warehouses and apartment blocks were at their most decrepit, coated with a deep screen of graffiti, image over language, language over image, cohered by the media of dirt and diesel oil, down to the ur-texts of protest, derision, and sexual obsession. Trains entering and leaving the Masarykovo and Hlavni Stations wailed on the sharp turns overhead, while lines of freight trucks congealed on the roads at ground level, the shoddy tarmac prized open or ground away to reveal the pitted old cobblestones underneath. After the final railway underpass, I turned left up a sharply inclined road towards the Žižkov Hill to escape that entanglement, ascending until the road expired into a pathway; up ahead, I could see the form of the derelict national monument, visible erratically through the pulses of sleet.

I had caught sight of that monument, poised on the opposite side of the city from the Hotel International and the Letná Plain, from the circling, stormbound airplane. While the statue of Stalin had been erased, the national monument still held its ground – it had been the largest monument in Europe up until the construction of Stalin's statue, and immediately took back that status at the instant of the statue's detonation. But this monument, too, was heading for erasure, with its emanation of permanent, infinite power now subject to cancellation at any moment; all that remained was to design an effective means of destruction. The monument's raw mix of histories and memories had become increasingly volatile, across the headlong course of the twentieth century, and was then casually nullified, with that monument's successively supplanted contents finally compacted together in their uniform obsolescence; the statue of the ferocious medieval warrior Jan Žižka had been constructed to embody nationalistic ambitions in the early years of the Czechoslovak state, while the immense marble cube directly behind it had then been adapted by the communist regime for its own glory, as a mausoleum for its embalmed leaders, from Klement Gottwald onwards, until a fire in the year following the destruction of Stalin's statue had incinerated those revered bodies, leaving only ashes. The facades of the mausoleum still held intricate metal friezes, showing the triumph of the Soviet armies in liberating Prague, their tanks and gesturing soldiers welcomed by its urban population with flowers; but many of the bronze figures of the soldiers had been ineptly rendered, and appeared monstrous, their faces convulsed and grimacing in their elation. Those metal friezes had now been half gouged away, for souvenirs or from anger, and the surfaces covered in graffiti tags.

The aged caretaker reluctantly opened up one of the monument's bronze doors, imprinted with fist-clenched peasants, for me to see inside, cursing at its weight; soon, he breathed, all this would be gone, and the tree-covered hill above the city would be a calm place for young people to run wild. Whatever came next, in all events, for that erased site, would be a savage rectifier, opening the ground for the next obsession of Europe. Inside, the only illumination for the vast, high-ceilinged space came from fluorescent tubing so encased in solidified dust that it hardly broke the darkness. But darkness itself is a content that reveals, and darkness forms a site where memory can't help exposing itself. The forms of trestle tables and stalls, once used for the sale of mementoes to visitors to the dead, were themselves as moribund as those I had glimpsed through the barred doors below Stalin's statue. I could make out the dais where the embalmed bodies had been displayed, and on the damp-streaked walls, the soiled outlines surrounding empty space where banners and pennants had exclaimed the resilience and immovability of power. I took a few steps across the floor, breathing tainted dust, but it held obstacles at ground level: debris, broken glass, sodden paper, and the caretaker cursed again, telling me I had seen enough, it was time to close the door again, it was over.

13

The descent back into the city from the Žižkov Hill was a vertiginous fall, feet sliding through black ice, my vision still haunted by the interior space of that frozen mausoleum and its hold upon the city, as though the wretched final traces of totalitarian power, in their void suspension above time, still somehow surreptitiously engulfed that city, permeating and determining the forms of its avenues and its inhabitants' gestures. Through its cancellation, that power appeared to have grown more virulent than during the decades when it had been enacted with regularity and banality upon the city; it seemed able now, from its subterranean position, to inflect with perverse ferocity that city's consumer frenzies, and to seize the oblivious children who had grown out of its moment of erasure. Those part-destroyed emanations of power, scattered over the city, stripped of their pure visibility but still seeping a lethal content, appeared dangerously mutable, ineradicable in the impact they wielded upon the city, as its nodal black holes. However marginal and forgotten they seemed, in their growing dereliction, those sites still absorbed and embodied the engrained historical fracture-lines of Europe, able to pinion and subjugate everything they touched. It would take the obliteration of every last trace of that immovable history to nullify its power – and then that city could free-fall, along with the entirety of Europe, down into a state of utter bliss, sensorially and historically liberated.

I headed south through the junctions of railway tracks and highways at the foot of the Žižkov Hill, down the Wilsonova ring road and past the ornate entrance to the original concourse of the Hlavni Station, as fast as I could go, without stopping, for hours, pulled on by those roaring avenues, distorting the habitual shape of my circuiting of the city, until I reached its southern fringes and the vast housing-block estates of Modřany. All the way south, along pavements of broken-glass shards, in clouds of gasoline fumes, it felt as though any kind of impetus, any form of momentum, must be valid, heart pumping with each awry step, as a way to cut into the city, to map it at speed; but by the time I reached the central plaza of Modřany, at the fall of night, I was exhausted and slumped down alongside the alcoholic and countercultural inhabitants of that plaza's graffiti'd concrete benches. The plaza was surrounded on each side by brittle ten-story apartment towers, constructed in the early 1970s, the windows illuminated fitfully at that twilight moment, each tower with a line of supermarkets and low-grade utilities stores at its foot. And at the summit of each of the four towers, a vast digital image-screen had been installed over the late 1990s, facing inwards to the plaza's center, replacing the now-vanished hoardings which had previously exhorted the population of those towers to support the communist state industries; but only one of the four screens was still functioning, repeatedly transmitting a digital animation lauding a hypermarket complex located somewhere beyond the city's edge, the fragile pixels blurring and scintillating in the evening light. The other three screens had already been abandoned, or had terminally malfunctioned, at some point in the last years, falling as instantly obsolete as the hoardings which had preceded them, and as the light faded, the three unilluminated surfaces swallowed the darkness and transmitted that instead.

As soon as it became night, the atmosphere in the plaza abruptly veered into violence, and I walked to the southern end of Modřany and crossed the district's arterial road to the tram terminus; too exhausted to complete the entirety of my circuit to the Smíchovské Station and then to the Letná Plain on foot, I waited instead for the tram which would take me back up the Vltava River valley to the railway bridge alongside the Smíchov district. Young women, born around the moment of the city's transformation, were now emerging from the towers, one by one, dressed for work in the sex clubs and pornography industries of the city's center. They took their places in the tram's interior and it jolted away, heading directly west towards the river, leaving the glowing Modřany towers behind; at the riverbank, it turned northwards, along the Vltava's eastern bank. A succession of derelict factories and chemical plants filled the narrow space between the tram tracks and the river for the first minutes of the journey, the gray armatures of steel sheeting peeling unstuck from the concrete core of the constructions.

The tram stopped at the railway bridge and I got off, leaving the other passengers to head on into the center of the city. A narrow footway ran alongside the northern edge of the bridge, across to the Smíchov district; the river swirled around the iron stanchions, heading north too, and the night express to Mariánské Lázně was slowly crossing, east to west, its passengers peering out from the rawly lit windows for a last vision of the city. I turned away from them to follow their eyes, as they gazed on the vanishing city.

14

On the tenth day of circling the city, I took a detour through its heart, exiting the Masarykovo Station and heading southwest towards the Bartolomějská Convent, where I had watched, a week or so before, the dispossessed inhabitants of the city's core waiting to be handed a chunk of rye bread from a grille in the wall, some of them vanishing back instantly into the city's dense alleyways, others remaining outside the convent to intersperse their consumption of the bread with pre-dawn swallows of pure spirit alcohol. This time, I went inside the convent's buildings and descended to cellar level, where the city's secret police had interrogated and tortured dissidents during the communist era, converting the Franciscan nuns' cells into cells for incarceration after the confiscation of the buildings in 1949. The convent had been returned to its previous occupants only after the events of 1989, some of the buildings wrecked, others gutted in the turmoil of that moment. I walked through the bare corridors, passing the succession of doorways to the cells. In order to generate income for renovations to the dilapidated buildings, those stone-floored torture cells had been converted into rooms for young travelers to the city, though the nuns were so averse to handling sums of money that the fees demanded from the travelers proved negligible, and parts of the convent buildings remained in a semi-ruinous and abandoned state, some of them frozen at the moment when the secret police had fled. Even the torture cells had received minimal renovation, with the torture instruments, restraints, and chairs simply replaced by three-level iron bunk beds covered by harsh blue blankets, where the young Estonian and Romanian travelers – the only ones sufficiently poverty-stricken to be tempted by the severe austerity of the place – spent nights of turbulent dreams.

I took a cell for the night from the young nun who supervised the building, paying the minuscule sum in advance and receiving a strict prohibition against smoking and drinking alcohol, together with the unwieldy iron key to the cell. On the walls of the nun's office, photographs from the early 1990s had been pinned, showing the inhabitants of the building who had survived their incarceration or torture, now visiting that space after it had been returned to the nuns' ownership; in those images, the human figures, dressed formally in smart suits, gazed at the desolate corridors and the building's blank facade, cast abruptly through transformed time into identical space. I took the stairway back down to the building's cellar level, past a vending machine dispensing black coffee and bottles of mineral water. That night, I lay underground on the uppermost bunk of the cell, awake; the silent building was near-deserted, the solid exterior walls encased by a layer of snow, and surrounded by the darkness of the European night and the stars overhead. No other travelers arrived to occupy the empty bunks, though I could hear, through the non-functioning air-ventilation system that ran between the cells, the whispered voices of two young Romanians, devising and then revising a journey through Europe, delirious with elation at their escapade. No trace remained in that humming air of the tortured; time had shattered, flowing freely, taking away with it the human bodies that it had once pinioned in space, and leaving behind that space as one of airless dereliction, too suffocating to be remade from zero, too ground-downwards into the subterranean detritus of Europe to breathe within.

In the early morning, the nuns were preoccupied with silently preparing the rye bread and soup to be disgorged through the grille in the building's foyer; the queue of embattled figures already snaked across the front windows of the building. Identical rye bread chunks had been laid out for the cells' few guests, together with a glass bowlful of pulped apples to signal the luxurious gulf that separated them from the figures outside. It seemed as though that moment of waiting and survival could continue indefinitely, poised at the furthest point that the body and the eye could bear. As I left the convent, its vast wooden entrance-door slammed behind me, shutting down that night spent with the remnants of torture, and I walked through the city's comatose heart, breathing deeply all the way back to the Masarykovo Station to resume my journey's suspended circuit.

15

Human life had been a complete accident, in the first place, in Europe: the tribes that began to inhabit that terrain and establish its civilization, 7,000 years before, entering it from the east and southeast, had considered it to be blighted and bedeviled, and had only reluctantly decided to cross the Ural and Carpathian mountains to settle in it. Africa was a much better prospect, and they considered the enticing options of other, unknown continents. But out of aberration, they went on into Europe. In the caves of river valleys, those invaders encountered several scattered communities of primitive people, whose origin was obscure, and who could think of nothing better to do with their time than to incise images of vulvas and livestock onto the walls of their dank caves. In most cases, the invaders simply slaughtered them in order to put an end to that devilish occupation. Later, wars broke out constantly on that continent, and fires spread through every city, destroying them utterly as soon as they were built, as though to demonstrate that those invaders had been correct in their initial assessment. On one occasion, an authoritarian power based on the eastern edge of Europe grasped the entire eastern lands of the continent and rendered their inhabitants subject to a capricious regime in which vast monuments were revered, only for that initiative to be abruptly overturned, and the same lands seized by a satanic trade cartel based on the western edge of Europe; the liberated inhabitants began to celebrate the onset of their new masters' power, but before long, that euphoria turned to dismay. Simultaneously, advances in scientific knowledge determined that the inhabitants of Europe would shortly no longer die, and would live forever, in their denudation, but that the entire continent would soon be immersed by the oceans and disappear at last, as a consequence of pollution-fueled climatic change; only the still-frozen lands of Antarctica – where the invaders should have originally headed – would any longer be habitable for the human species.

On the twentieth day of circuiting the city, pivoting around its railway stations and increasingly taking detours through its annex spaces of concrete-block estates, I came to an abrupt end point to that obsessional maneuver. The concourses of the railway stations had begun to blur into one another, and I could no longer distinguish between the alcoholic or drug-dealing vagrants stalled in those spaces and the passengers rushing through to the platforms to make their legitimate journeys across the central European lands. The memory of the previous days' circuits vanished in my exhaustion, then any memory of my life prior to that centrifugal movement around and above the city also evanesced, and I was left only with the awareness of the immediacy of my body, in the act of inhabiting the city. One morning, standing still in the lower concourse of the Hlavni Station, within the cacophony of train announcements and the rapid crisscrossing of human figures, I realized that my own memory had been drained away by that circuiting of the city, canceled so thoroughly that I could now begin to move through the void center of Europe and to allow its own memory, or the fragments of memory that survived there, to inhabit me. That circuiting ended and I was expelled still more deeply into the heart of Europe.

I decided to spend the entirety of that winter traversing the cities of central Europe, attempting to locate an image or human body that engulfed and transmitted the memory of Europe, as I had envisaged in Los Angeles, just over twenty days before. On a café table under the imperial dome of the Hlavni Station's original concourse, I drew an itinerary at speed across a map of Europe torn from a magazine, tracing pencil-arrows at random through the empty gaps between cities: Budapest, Linz, Kraków, Vienna, Bratislava, Brno, determining the course of that journey without reflection, compulsively skimming the pencil over the surface space of Europe, and aware that any such mapping imposed on that surface would inevitably rectify itself into a set of diversions, deviations, pitfalls, descents and elevations. Nothing was discernible from ground level, where those cities appeared stultified and absent; instead, any vision of Europe was located overhead and in its subterranea, in movements through its altitudes and its ash-and-cinder skies, and through trackings of its urban underpasses and concealed spaces. As soon as the map of my itinerary was complete, I crumpled it in my fist, letting the nicks in my fingernails tear the paper, then carefully spread it out again, its surface now indented with a new landscape of rips, folds and furrows, the pencil lines linking the cities of Europe blurred and disjointed. That was the map I would follow.

Outside the café, the icy rain was beating down on the cars heading along the Wilsonova ring road, and the leaking dome overhead dripped water over its faded frescoes of central European cities, painted in 1909, before the following decade of imperial warfare transformed those cities, erasing and annulling some of them entirely, and unexpectedly elevating others to momentary grandeur. I picked out the near-dissolved frescoes of Budapest, Linz, Kraków, Vienna, Bratislava and Brno among the forms of other cities that had corroded illegibly within engine soot and dirt. Seven hours remained until the departure of the night express to Budapest.

16

All through that night, on the train from Prague to Budapest, the interrogation and torture cells of the Bartolomějská Convent continued to haunt me; staring out in exhaustion into the Slovakian forests and illuminated factory-zones, that subterranean space kept impacting into my memory, flashing momentarily and then dying away again. By the time the journey expired at Budapest's Keleti Station, I felt as though I had undergone some kind of assault of memory, conducted with rhythmic acetylene pressure against the background of the central European night. The afterburn of those memory-flashes still overlayered my vision as I gazed around the station, already densely inhabited at dawn with its eager population of hustlers, conveyors and intermediators, ready to deal any corporeal or financial product. In order to counterbalance my night spent in the Bartolomějská Convent's corridor of interrogation cells, I had decided to head immediately on arriving in Budapest to the former secret police building, where that city's dissidents had been tortured and covertly shot during the communist era. But where Prague's interrogation center had been located in the decrepit basement of a damp-seeping convent, its counterpart in Budapest possessed far more luxurious surroundings, housed in the Adria Palace, a vast marble-clad building constructed as the prestigious headquarters of an insurance company, in the same year as the cities of Europe had been painted onto the Hlavni Station's imperial dome. After the fall of the Hungarian communist regime, the Adria Palace had lain empty for over a decade, in one of the city's central squares, emanating too virulent a charge to be touched or transformed. I would walk past it on winter nights in the early 1990s, its foyer barred and grilled, the guard's table inside still bearing the register that had recorded the moment of arrival of every entrant to that now-glacial space. The building's glowing white-marble facade remained pristine, aberrantly unmarked by the graffiti exclamations that coated every other surface of the city during those years, but the uniform darkness of that rectangular building's long rows of windows still transmitted a muted language of scars to the city around it; it was a building of raw ghosts, talking without tongues or teeth. Despite my best efforts, there was never a way to get inside. In time, that tainted aura gradually evanesced, and a French property corporation eventually bought and cursorily gutted the building, retaining its original facade and staircases intact, but tearing out every ceiling and interior wall, and jettisoning the entire contents of the dust-encrusted interrogation rooms and offices, before finally reopening the building as the city's most lavish hotel.

I took a room for the night from the multilingual reception-
ist, whose smile had been designed to placate even the most
irascible of Balkan or Baltic entrepreneurs at the discovery that
the cost of the hotel's lush suites matched the annual average
income in their own cities. Digital screens arranged discreetly
around the foyer provided information on financial market
flux. Empty space soared upwards above the central staircase,
where floor upon floor of offices had been demolished, towards
a roof indented with golden stars; the immense hotel suites
had been constructed on all four sides of the building, along
granite walkways overlooking the foyer of black-leather sofas
below, where gorgeous white-blond prostitutes, internationally
renowned for their ability to masturbate their clients rapidly to
ecstasy with their sleek toes and heels, scanned the fluctuating
retinal responses of passing hotel guests with minute facial
movements. I followed every walkway of the building's six
floors, past suites that ascended in scale and luxury with every
story, but no residue whatsoever remained of the building's
previous incarnation; its carapace had been so comprehensively
emptied out, like that of a slaughtered animal, that any trace of
that space of interrogation had been rendered void. Even in the
basement gymnasium, where businessmen in leisurewear were
grunting with commitment over cardiac-exertion-propelled
machinery, all marks and exhalations of torture had vanished.
Time had accelerated to such a degree in that space, calibrated
in a ferocious collision of financial, sexual and digital rates
of expenditure, that it had concertina'd into a single frozen
moment.

Late that night, I stood on the balcony of my suite, wearing
a sumptuous red bathrobe imprinted with the Adria Palace
Hotel insignia, and looked out over the Erzsébet Tér square.
In the park directly below, small-scale furtive drug-dealing

was going on among the trees; a few taxis sped up and down the boulevard on the eastern side of the square, and I could hear the faint sound of a woman singing, somewhere, but otherwise, there was silence. Like every guest of that hotel, I had supplanted the space of the suppressed or tortured; even the torturers and their bureaucrats had been dismissed, too, and had disappeared without trace. A flood of luxurious oblivion now saturated that space so thoroughly that, for that night, at least, the reapparition of memory would be an accursed event.

17

In that city of headlong financial desire, where the residue of the decades of communism had been ostensibly expunged or displaced, Stalin remained the urgent subject matter. On the morning after my first night in the Adria Palace Hotel, sitting in the lavishly chandelier'd breakfast-room that now occupied the antechamber space where prisoners had once awaited their turn to enter the building's interrogation rooms, I read a front-page newspaper article with the headline: "Budapest No to Stalin." The first paragraph announced: "Former Soviet dictator, Josef Stalin, is unworthy of the title of honorary citizen of Budapest, therefore the Budapest City Council does not consider him one, according to a draft resolution prepared by members of parliament. The resolution nullifies the 1947 election of the dictator as an honorary citizen." Such outright desire for Stalin's negation in the city appeared to signal an intense passion that could overturn itself at any moment, and that former interrogation space itself seemed to risk an inverse transformation, with the breakfasting Austrian entrepreneurs, earnestly finalizing plans for out-of-town hypermarkets, in danger of being cursorily expelled from their leather banquettes, and that space reconstructed in preparation for the instigation of new tortures, new suppressions. Any former Europe, however energetically obliterated, still forms a vital splinter in the heart of contemporary Europe.

For many years, that city's inhabitants had been working to decimate history, along with the human bodies that carried that history, but had been left with its presence still more burningly projected into their eyes. I left the breakfast room and walked through the roaring morning boulevards to the Hungarian film archive, to watch the film images of the destruction of Stalin's statue during the 1956 Budapest uprising, three years after his death. Those film fragments prefigured and had set the course for innumerable subsequent topplings and assaults upon statues, from those executed throughout eastern Europe around the end of the 1980s, through to the 2003 uprooting of the shoddy statue of Saddam Hussein, with its fragile interior core of iron-piping and cement, that had marked the American army's seizure of Baghdad. In the archive's minuscule screening room, the grumbling technicians laced up the 16 mm images from battered gray film-cans and turned on the rickety projector. The uprising's participants had felled the eighty-foot-high statue from its site on the Dózsa György Út avenue, on the northeastern edge of the city's center, and had then roped Stalin's head and dragged the statue down into the city's heart, at night, along the wide Andrássy Út avenue, with a great concerted human effort, many hundreds strong, as though engaged in a belated variant of some vast Neolithic construction project; they reached the central Bajcsy-Zsilinszky Út boulevard, within sight of the Adria Palace's windows, and then meticulously shattered that statue with hammers into thousands of stone fragments. Those bursts of film images were scratched and indistinct, each sequence only eight or ten seconds in length, as though they belonged to the very origins of cinema. As they pulled the statue along, in darkness, the uprising's participants appeared concentrated on their work of destruction to the exclusion of all elation; flashes of light ignited behind them from the surrounding buildings. In the final image, the statue's still-roped head had been broken off, and the film camera focused in on Stalin's unconcerned face. That uprising would shortly be savagely ended.

Only Stalin's statue had been broken apart; when the remainder of the city's communist monuments became redundant, over thirty years later, they were transported out to the city's southwestern periphery to form a "statue Park," the bronze and steel statues mounted on substandard red-brick pedestals and arranged in six interlocking circles around a red star incised into the park's grass, with the statues of Lenin and Hungarian communist leaders placed alongside figures of heroically gesturing workers and friezes of young pioneers in action. Only Stalin was absent. After I had left the film archive, I tracked the course of that uprooted statue down the Andrássy Út avenue, past an annex-building of the Adria Palace, which had been transformed from a subsidiary interrogation center into a commercial museum devoted to the victims of twentieth-century totalitarian regimes, fascism and communism now blithely scrambled together into an inextricable morass of memory, until I reached the Bajcsy-Zsilinszky Út junction where Stalin's statue had been destroyed. Every human figure and vehicle in the city appeared to be amassing upon that point, as though it were irresistibly attracting all of the elements necessary for a salutary urban implosion. I headed outwards to the city's peripheries, towards the Statue Park, via a screeching tram that reeled over the pitted streets, through endless swathes of abandoned factory buildings and the debris of chemical complexes, past the facades of post-communist sex clubs now boarded-up, their names – Coco-Bongo Klub, Big Fuck Klub – graffiti'd into near-illegibility after those clubs' clientele of factory-workers had become obsolete, vanishing into the alcoholic exit-zones of the city.

When the Statue Park had first opened, in 1993, it was still surrounded by countryside seamed with hiking trails, but in the following years, suburban shopping malls and prefabricated houses grew up densely around it. As I approached the park, I could hear the sound of revolutionary songs blaring out of the speakers positioned around its ticket office, but the site was almost empty, its pathways waterlogged and the red star at its center faded away. The pedestals had been constructed so shoddily that the heavy statues gradually crushed their brick supports, so that the figures of Lenin and Comrade Ostapenko had now begun to veer wildly, their heroic gestures sent awry against the background of the corporate shopping malls and suburban housing. It was only from a far distance, from the waste ground of discarded washing machines and stunted scrubland behind the Statue Park, that those gestures could be glimpsed in isolation, still poised, in incomprehensible corporeal tension and triumph, against a vast sky of dark clouds.

18

I stayed on at the Adria Palace, determined to remain in that hotel until the city had finally removed Stalin from its list of honorary citizens, and had succeeded in executing a wounding or suturing of its history: any act performed on that livid memory simultaneously cut and healed it. In the meantime, the lavish sensorial space of the hotel engulfed me, and I sat for days on end in the lobby and bar, watching the intricate negotiations and strategies of the new masters of Europe as they cemented deals over bottles of vintage champagne and Stolichnaya vodka; I began compulsively to envisage my own designs for lustrous corporate towers, surmounted by high-definition image-screens transmitting exclamatory digital loops, and to contemplate the unassailable human benefits of out-of-town hypermarkets and of vast hoardings erected along urban arterial roads. I started to feel at home. But that extirpation of Stalin failed to materialize; after a few days, I read in a further newspaper report that the striking-out of his name had now been put on indefinite hold: it seemed that act had already been anticipated for several decades, and would undoubtedly remain under discussion for at least several more. I reluctantly decided to cut short my stay at the Adria Palace, and to head deeper into the heart of Europe.

Caught within the axis of the city's financial and media district, a liberation memorial still stood to the Soviet soldiers who had seized Budapest from its German occupiers in 1945, reducing large elements of it to a flattened terrain of debris in the process. On my final walk through the city, I circled the high wire fencing which had been set up around the monument to protect it from assault; guards in all-black uniforms circled round the other side of the fence, ineptly slapping their truncheons in menace against their thighs and whistling at their slavering guard-dogs, whose boxes of food were propped up against the monument's column. The entirety of its text had been torn from that monument, rendering it adrift and perversely mute in the otherwise densely inscribed and voluble city, though the gold Soviet star poised above its summit remained intact, outlined

51

against the ornate, gilded facade of the Inter-Europa Bank behind it.

From that locked-down space at the city's core, I headed upwards, across the Danube, climbing to the summit of the sheer Gellért-Hegy hill, where the city's other Soviet liberation memorial stood: the vast bronze figure of a robed woman, holding a palm branch over her head, at full stretch, as a gesture of adulation at the Soviet forces' arrival. Naked figures carrying fire towards the city remained positioned at either side of the monument's plinth, but the statue of a flag-wielding Soviet soldier that had originally accompanied the outstretched woman, a sten-gun strapped around his shoulder, had been uprooted, dispatched to its place in the Statue Park on the city's periphery; the text on the monument's plinth had been ripped away here too, the faint border of rust corrosion around the missing Soviet star now encompassing empty space, and the sides of that plinth layered instead with residues of graffiti'd condemnations. The city and the river stretched out far below, north and south, their outer edges effaced in the ice-cohered pollution haze. Groups of schoolchildren kept arriving at the summit, groaning at the long exertion of the climb, before recovering their breath sufficiently to emulate the statue's stance for photographs, their arms stretched upwards too, in the rarefied air, their faces solemn with cold laughter. Those children's gestures exactly matched the incoherence of the statues' gestures I had glimpsed from the wasteland behind the Statue Park, all of them subtracted from their histories. But high above Europe, any gesture, however exhausted or drained, irresistibly sifts and reactivates traces of memory from oblivion, and launches those traces onward to other sites, poised above other cities, across the center of Europe, until that incoherence melts away, and a new body or gesture takes form.

19

From the liberation memorial, I headed away from the city, walking towards the densely wooded hills on its western edge, along pathways between luxurious villas constructed at precariously tilted angles to the city below. While the light above the Gellért-Hegy hill had been pristine, tainted only by the pollution haze rising from the traffic-saturated boulevards below, the woodland air grew sodden with fog as I ascended: the villa facades were opaque behind vertical sheets of mist, and the ripped tarmac below my feet breathed out a thick white vapor. My lungs filled with pulses of iced moisture as I kept going upwards, until the pathway abruptly leveled out onto a plateau of open parkland, with the outline of a railway station just visible through the fog, behind communist-era statues of uniformed children engaged in strenuous outdoor activities.

Inside the railway station, uniformed children of around fourteen were solemnly preparing the next train for departure; on the walls of the concourse, vast painted murals showed the construction of the railway, between 1948 and 1952, by dedicated groups of young pioneers, whose successors had now inherited the stations and track, which ran for twenty miles through the hills to the northwest of the city. It had been built by the hands of those children of a zero-level, slaughterhouse Europe, at a time when Budapest itself still lay largely decimated, pounded to dust by the battles between Soviet and German armies in the final period of the Second World War. Although the railway had been conceived during the communist era, and dedicated to the glory of Stalin, it had survived intact the communist regime's collapse, the contemporary pioneers still dressed in their smart royal-blue uniforms, the girls and the boys together, their dutiful determination undiminished, standing in line to salute the arrival and departure of every train, on its journey from nowhere to nowhere, as a major commemorative event.

On that evening of engulfing fog, I was alone on the train apart from three Ukrainian women from Odessa, on their day off from the arduous corporeal demands of the Budapest sex industry, hunched together in the corner of the carriage to perfect their make-up, oblivious to the journey. The train rumbled into the forest, threading through the hills to the highest point above the city, the fog pressing in, rendering the surroundings invisible and silent; the air cleared only for one moment, when the train climbed above the upper limit of the fog, slicing up into sunlight, and the line of waiting pioneers at the János-hegy station appeared as illuminated ghosts. The train moved on; every few minutes, it passed small clusters of pioneers at the trackside, charged with ensuring its safe passage. On its descent towards the Hűvösvölgy terminus, it passed through a long black tunnel, and at the midpoint, on either side of the train, I could see the figures of saluting pioneers, standing in narrow recesses in the tunnel's dripping darkness, holding hand-torches to alert the train's driver and passengers to their reassuring presence. In their airless, lightless isolation, infinitely far from the immediate consumer frenzies of the city's center, those lost children of contemporary Europe still marked with somber dedication the aberration of its history. But on the return journey, in darkening fog, on the last train of the evening passing through stations embedded deep in the forest, I saw rebellious children too, their uniforms askew and their duty unstuck, subversively distorting their salutes into gestures of obscene derision at the futility of their own archaic spectacle, or at the passengers witnessing it.

Back at the now-empty station where the pioneer railway began, I left that world behind and headed back down to the city, to catch a night train out of Budapest. I passed below the fog's ceiling, halfway down the hillside of villas; the darkness had come down, and the city now burned below. As I descended, the villas ended and the tenements began. I traversed the center of Budapest, across the Danube, to the main Keleti Station; throughout the city, the buildings' image-screens and hoardings had been illuminated for the night. That strange site of memory, up in the hills, had been obliterated, propelled out of my eyes and mind by the furor of the city. And to remember at all involves the transformation of any site or human body into a raw, manipulable image. The city is the great amasser and eraser of such images, operating at such velocity that, from time to time, it appears that the city is all images, or that its surface is so blurred by speed into habituation that it holds no images at all – and that incandescent surface is so dense with the traces of all of its annulled or discarded memories that they are now invisible.

20

I entered the Keleti Station through the underpass beneath its grandiose facade of glass and marble, visible all the way from the Danube along the haywire Rákóczi Út avenue. Bodies were pressed together in urgent chaos in that circular underpass, used by inhabitants of all of the surrounding districts to traverse a space uncrossable at ground level, where the traffic rotated in non-stop flux, the drivers too compelled by speed ever to countenance any threat of gridlock, moving under unseen hoardings and image-screens installed on the roofs of multistory fast-food outlets and sex clubs. The inhabitants of that underpass attempted to make direct horizontal transits,

each one thrown askew by the irregular pulses of violent movement towards opposed exits; simultaneously, great disruptive
bursts of bodies emerged vertically from the underground
station beneath the underpass, so that any successful crossing
of that subterranea had to be lithely executed, in a headlong
scrambling of direction.

The Keleti Station formed a fluctuating space at the edge
of Europe's heart. Although the trains exiting that station initially headed due east, away out of that heart, in the direction
of Istanbul and Kishinev, they perversely twisted back after
a minute or two, as though outmaneuvering any potential
escapees from Europe; they then crossed the Danube and
abruptly headed west, back towards that engulfing heart. The
station marked the seething crossing point for Europe's exiles,
its arena mastered by brokers of human bodies. Although most
travelers from the eastern lands arrived in that city by bus rather
than train, after sleepless nights crammed upright on ripped
plastic seating, they headed immediately for the Keleti Station
in any case, drawn by its aura of being able to propel those
new inhabitants of the city onwards, for a fee, in a centrifugal
distribution that would unfailingly dispatch their bodies to the
exact location in Europe they had dreamed about and desired.
Those expulsions sent them flying over the entire terrain of
Europe. But at their impact zones, those exiles invariably found
themselves in locations profoundly mismatched with their
originating dreams of Europe, at its far opposite corner to the
one they had envisaged, or dislocated even at its heart.

The worst moment to arrive at the Keleti Station was at dawn,
as I had done on this journey, when the all-night frenzy of that
distribution and allocation of human bodies was reaching its
point of sheer exhaustion, and the faces of the contracted or
prostituted had become hollowed with anxiety or boredom. But

in the evening, as the final trains began to fill with passengers and to prepare for departure, that night-work was only just beginning. On the side-platforms under the station's elevated iron canopy, vents exuded gusts of hot steam from unfathomable underground sources; it mercifully warmed the legs of the frozen passengers boarding late-running one-carriage trains for the rural border towns of southern Hungary. From those platforms, I could see figures moving in the decrepit, peeling tenements directly adjoining the south side of the station, their rooms unshuttered: people eating around tables under bare lightbulbs, preparing for bed, or leaning out of their windows, stilled and indifferent, smoking cigarettes as they watched the turmoil of departure.

On the crowded international platforms, families were loading swathes of suitcases and containers onto the four or five departing trains. Every language ever spoken on the planet was being uttered; even languages designed to be enunciated at a leisurely pace were being spat out at speed. I chose a train at random, without looking at the destination board, entrusting it to take me further into the heart of Europe. The train left the darkened city behind, duly pivoting after a few moments and heading into the west. I could see nothing at all through the window; it seemed that the fog that had earlier covered the pioneer railway's elevated route had now come down to obscure the entire western lands. So I remembered other journeys. One winter night, in 1989, I had taken an express train from the Keleti Station; on that occasion, the station had been strangely empty, its habitual populations too jarred, momentarily, by the transformations of the last months to effectively pursue their work. The night express, too, had been empty; it was the end of All Saints' Day, and the train roared past illuminated cemetery after cemetery that burned in the darkness, each grave marked by clusters of lighted candles. Every few minutes, the glow of another cemetery appeared, intensified, and vanished. I saw nothing of the surrounding provincial towns, erased or already shut down for the night. And between the apparitions of those cemeteries, there was nothing at all: only dense black night. The dead lit up a broken route, of wounds or elation, through Europe, traced by the rushing eye for a particle of a second.

21

I left that night express in the early-morning hours, in Linz, cast out into void space on the southwestern edge of central Europe. The train had left behind its screening pall of fog on the border with Austria. I took the first tram of the morning from the railway station, up through the city to the banks of the Danube. Although that city now possessed an aura of mundanity, in its contemporary form, at dawn, it had been envisioned seventy years earlier as the greatest of all European cities, modeled and planned for overhaul by Hitler, who viewed it as his home (he had been born in the countryside to the west of the city) and demanded its reconstruction as an extravagantly magnified variant of his favorite city, Budapest. Linz had been intended for transformation into the urban heart of Europe, into the determining site of all of its power and slaughter, as the "Führerstadt." Radial avenues of colonnaded government buildings and ministries, in red Swedish granite, would converge from both sides of the river on the axis of the city's bridge; Hitler himself designed a new bridge for the city, and sent teams of architects from Berlin to realize his plans, soon after his annexation of Austria in 1938. And in all of the countries occupied by Hitler's armies, art museums were relentlessly pillaged in the early 1940s in order for Linz to encompass the entirety of Europe's great art within the vast "Führermuseum"; the city's railway station was to be displaced far to the south in order to give maximal space for the colossal, domed building, well over a mile in diameter, that would hold those artworks, seized from every other European city. The Führermuseum would also incorporate space for an immense, infinite library, containing the original editions of every book ever printed (apart from those already burned by Hitler). Gigantic concert halls, opera houses and theaters would comprise concentric layers emanating from that sole site of European culture. The rest of Europe's cities, drained to exhaustion of power and art, would come to form subsidiary wastelands and transit zones to travel from and through, on the way to Linz; only the most supreme of Europe's elites would be allowed to inhabit the city's palatial apartment blocks, planned for construction along the Danube's banks. Many thousands of art works and rare books were cataloged and assigned for transportation to the Führermuseum in the months following Hitler's invasions, and only temporarily left in place until the Linz museum could be built at the conclusion of the Second World War; thousands more were confiscated, loaded onto trains and then stored in underground salt-mine caverns, in the isolated forests to the west of Linz, in anticipation of Hitler's victory and their eventual move to the city.

From the Danube, I walked back into the southern avenues of Linz. In that city of luxurious banality, the inhabitants were industriously at work, and I followed near-deserted tenement-building streets, running at rigid parallel distances to one another, calm and well ordered, each equipped with a succession of sex clubs and pornography stores, sucking in the few passers-by; the entire eastern city had become occupied by tracts of financial-service buildings and trade-fair halls, taking the place of now-derelict steelworks and chemical factories. The city had diffused into the anonymity of corporate Europe, gradually imploding at low velocity. Department stores lined the tram routes, each with a digital image-screen burning out images above its entrance, like a single cyclops eye, transmitting frenzied animations that lauded the concessions inside. In the city's central park, a few counterculture-inflected youths drinking raw alcohol signaled the only mark of deviance skewed across that homogenous urban facade, and as the light began to fail, carefully dressed teenagers filed determinedly into the city's only nightclub, the Kolosseum.

As the night fell, I decided to remain in the city, to look for any surviving traces of its notional elevation to the status of Europe's urban heart. I walked back to the city's medieval main square, the Hauptplatz, close to the Danube; Hitler's bridge bordered the square's northern face. On March 12, 1938, on a triumphal journey through Austria after an absence of over twenty years, Hitler had become so overcome with nostalgia for his childhood in Linz that he resolved capriciously to annex the country, instantly, rather than awaiting an apposite moment, as he had planned. After an evening at the city's ornate Traxlmeyer café, he returned to his hotel, the Wolfinger, a former monastery building on the Hauptplatz, appeared at the window of his room in the center of the second floor, and announced to a small but exultant crowd in the square outside that they were now citizens of Greater Germany; the following day, he pronounced the same message from the balcony of the Linz City Hall, applauded by a 50,000-strong audience, before moving on to Vienna to announce Austria's annexation to an even vaster crowd, from the balcony of the Habsburg imperial palace. I crossed the darkening Hauptplatz and found the

Wolfinger Hotel still there, facing the square's plague cross, its dilapidated pale-green facade carrying an incomplete assemblage of tattered European flags. The hotel was almost entirely empty, far too run down and unreconstructed to attract any of the city's elegant, laptop-wielding trade-fair clientele; from a free selection of the dust-encrusted rooms, I chose the one from whose window Hitler had addressed his new subjects. That night, I looked out on the Linz city square from that obsolete memory-portal into the massacred, annulled history of Europe.

22

I spent several weeks in the silent guest lounge at the Wolfinger Hotel, moving from one sawdust-stuffed leather sofa to another among the ceiling-high, century-old detritus of hunting trophies and peasant memorabilia, habituating myself to the apparent erasure of all traces of Hitler from the face of the city. Although Austria had undergone only a superficial denazification program in the late 1940s, in contrast to that imposed by its occupiers upon western Germany, the presence of Hitler's project for Linz as the new heart of Europe had been successfully expurgated at that time. The name of Hitler, and his plans for Linz's infinite expansion into grandeur, seemed to have been comprehensively wiped from the city and forgotten; its inhabitants appeared to have even embraced the cancellation of that too-deep upheaval in their provincial lives. Civic banners and posters throughout the city center now announced, in English, "Linz is Live." But, walking in the Hauptplatz, the destination sign of a tram abruptly entered my peripheral vision, and I misread the name "Hiller Strasse" as "Hitler

Strasse"; without thinking, I boarded the tram, in the aberrant delusion that it might be heading through some parallel vision of the city, into an oblivion-inflicted history. That tram was soon speeding through the southern suburbs, the impermeable corporate sheen of the city gradually splintering into streets of insalubrious bars and sex supermarkets, to terminate at a concrete-block satellite estate, where clusters of broken benches supported professional complainants and spirits-drinkers, profoundly disabused by their status in the city, or in Europe. Everywhere, I read the graffiti: "Linz ist Arsch."

In the mid 1970s, the city authorities of Linz had decided that it would become Europe's first "digital city," embedded forever into immediacy and into the contemporary; no one would then even think to recall Hitler's plans, or even be able to, within the insistent compulsion to build another kind of "city of the future," powered by engulfing digital images and computer megabytes. At that time, few people had even heard of digital technologies or computers, and those plans appeared a visionary innovation for the city. The world's first digital arts center, Ars Electronica, five stories high and made of concrete, was constructed in 1979 on the banks of the Danube, poised directly over the northeastern end of Hitler's bridge. For a time, it functioned in isolation from the rest of the city, its still-arcane exhibitions focusing on ways in which digital technologies could overhaul and reactivate the obsolete human species and its means of perception. Then, in the early 1990s, the department stores and finance complexes situated all along the avenue running directly south from the Danube bridge began to install their own large-format digital screens, of variable resolution, their erratic pixels flickering incessantly; the side-street businesses too began to set up rows of smaller image-screens, so that from the surrounding hills, the entire city at night now appeared as a skeletal arrangement, its spine and limbs cohered and illuminated by digital images, its throat formed by Hitler's bridge, and its tilted skull taking the shape of the Ars Electronica center, glowing in the darkness like an oblivious time-bomb.

Each morning and night, I exited the Wolfinger Hotel's monastic foyer to walk for hours in the city. Its three simultaneous existences had become so impacted in my mind that they were now impossible to disentangle: the digital city, the banal city of well-functioning, corporate mundanity, and the never-built city of looted grandeur and genocidal power that had been designed to form the pivotal site of Europe. None of them held any divine right to have ever been originated, nor to occupy that space in its contemporary moment, nor to be remembered, with affection or horror, in the future; but all three cities continually permeated and contaminated one another, effortlessly penetrating the fragile membranes of time and space, their traces flickering like blown pixels between visibility and invisibility and back again, amassing around my eyes and feet, with every step taken through that space. At the dead of night, I returned to Hitler's room in the Wolfinger Hotel.

23

From the Danube bridge, a path ran westwards alongside the southern riverbank, away from the city, past abandoned quays where the discontented Linz teenagers gathered at night; the stone faces of the remaining quayside stanchions had been decorated with inverted Christian crosses, satanic graffiti, and the word "genocide." The Danube was flowing fast and deep, slate-gray. I followed the pathway as it looped northwards. A densely wooded hill rose directly from the riverbank, with a steep path winding up from the Danube to its summit. I could see the tower of a brick-built folly on that summit, just visible between the trees, and behind it, on the highest elevation point over the city, rows of antennae transmitted television and cellphone signals to the inhabitants of Linz. I began my ascent.

An hour later, I reached the summit; up there, the exhaled rushes of air through the cedars were the only sound. Hitler had formulated plans for the future of his own body in Linz, alongside his project to transform that city into the originating site for the future of Europe itself (and retrospectively to accord Linz the status of the mystical location of Europe's birth). On the summit of that hill, the Freidberg, he had planned to build his retirement home, to which he would withdraw, after his work had been accomplished, Europe utterly subjugated to him, to await death. While the city below expanded into triumphal grandeur, embodying unbreakable power and amassing all of Europe's art into its vast museum, Hitler would watch that urban mutation from the Freidberg, as his own body disintegrated into terminal ruination and death. From the mid 1930s, he drew innumerable plans for that retirement home, incorporating the existing tower into his designs. Many of his sketches were bound into leather volumes, in anticipation of their imminent realization, and stored for wartime safekeeping alongside the great art works of Europe, in the salt-mine caverns to the west of Linz; but Hitler kept other designs for that retirement home with him in his Berlin bunker, together with his plans for the great metamorphosis of Linz itself, and pored endlessly over them in the spring months of 1945, in the last moment of his life, as the Soviet army advanced towards him.

The Danube valley directly below the Freidberg gathered and channeled winter storms into the city, and a storm was now coming in. I climbed to the top of the tower, constructed by the Linz "Association for Beauty" in 1888, the year before Hitler's birth, to commemorate the Habsburg Emperor Franz Josef I's first forty years in power; at one point, a cubicle had been installed at the tower's base for the collection of admission fees, but it had been abandoned, long ago, its surface then saturated with graffiti layers, and the rare visitors to the Freidberg's summit were now free to ascend the tower's precipitous wooden stairway at will. The viewing platform at the top was open to the elements; I sheltered at the top of the stairway until the fast-moving storm of rain and hail had whipped over, and the air grew clear in every direction. The serrated Austrian mountain ranges rose up in the southwest; to the north and east, hills of a slightly smaller elevation to that of the Freidberg encircled the city's suburbs. That entire city spread out below the Freidberg, every avenue and building, without exception, visible from this elevation, with Hitler's bridge in its dead center.

Hitler had envisaged his own death taking place on the Freidberg, following his contented retirement: the death of an exhausted but victorious warrior. During that retirement, a vast bell-tower was to have been constructed on the northern bank of the Danube, in full view of the Freidberg, to house his body. The bell-tower was to be located alongside his bridge, in the area of Linz known as Urfahr, on the site now occupied by the Ars Electronica digital center, with a gigantic porphyry base, able both to support the tower's weight and to resist the Danube floods. Just over a mile in height, the tower was designed to hold Hitler's body, encased in granite, at its very summit, directly over a set of immense bells perpetually chiming works by his favorite composers, at extreme volume, non-stop, enough to wake the dead, and forever imprinting his memory, sonically and visually, on the entire population of Linz. At that time, the tower's height would have far surpassed every building ever constructed in Europe, or the world; since then, only contemporary Japanese architects, such as Arata Isozaki, the self-proclaimed advocate of "impossible" and "unbuildable" utopian architecture, destined for cities already in ruins, have ever conceived of towers of such scale. But Hitler's death took place elsewhere, his half-incinerated body clumsily dissected by the Soviet forces, in a hastily assembled pathology laboratory in the town of Buch, to the north of Berlin, the detritus of bones then shunted haphazardly around eastern Germany in an ammunition crate, in the postwar chaos, before being tipped into a hole in the ground, and concreted over, in the backyard of a rubbish-collection company in the suburbs of Magdeburg, and then finally dug up in 1970 in order to be incinerated once again, down to the last ash.

I stood for a moment longer on that viewing platform, watching a more violent storm appear in the distance, on its way from the western skies; then I looked down again on the city. From the Freidberg, a colossal phantom city of towers, extravagant monuments, and Europe-encompassing museums now irresistibly supplanted itself for a second, in my eyes, over the contemporary city that actually lay below, with its well-ordered networks of finance centers and its run-down concrete-block estates on the urban peripheries. That mundane city could be erased without loss from the face of Europe; few people would even notice its vanishing. But when I closed my eyes and looked down again, that city had obstinately reappeared. It was Hitler's monstrous city, instead, that had been utterly forgotten; that city down below now absorbed and dispelled every last hallucination of Europe's heart.

24

From the Freidberg, I took the path back down into the city; an hour later, I was standing on the center of Hitler's bridge. The tarmac on all four traffic lanes remained wet from the storms that had passed over the city, and the sets of tram tracks running down the center of the bridge now glittered in lackluster sunlight. Below the eastern parapet, Danube cruise ships with names in Cyrillic characters had been moored for the winter. It was a quiet moment in the day, the assiduous inhabitants of Linz confined within their financial-services buildings. Few figures crossed the bridge on foot. For several hours, I searched every granite surface of the bridge for any trace of its role as the pivotal site of Hitler's ever-escalating reformulation of that city, and of his conception of Europe with that bridge at its very core. The bridge bore no text. Only the spraycan graffiti directly beneath its southern end, on the granite wall alongside the sheltered, beerbottle-strewn Danube pathway, incised that history: "One Hitler is Enough," and "Death to the Architects," though those exclamations had faded, and meshed almost to illegibility with innumerable other graffiti detailing the sexual obsessions and attributes of the young nocturnal inhabitants of that dank, urine-tainted space.

From its origins, Hitler had conceived of a rarefied status for that bridge, naming it the "Nibelungen-Brücke," marking the location where, in the mythical *Nibelungenlied*, the character of Kriemhild crossed the Danube. Work on the bridge began in September 1938, six months after Hitler had stayed at the Wolfinger Hotel on his journey to annex Austria, and finally ended in 1943. Hitler had instructed that only granite of supreme quality and endurance be used in its construction, and his teams of architects, led by Fritz Tamms and Karl Schächterle, scoured the quarries of central Europe for the required materials; the vast blocks for the bridge's supporting pillars came from the quarries of the nearby concentration camp of Mauthausen. Although Hitler had designed the bridge himself, repeatedly, down to the last ornate detail, with castellated turrets at both ends and a soaring steel arch above its span, his architects methodically amended the designs, rendering the bridge far wider in scale than Hitler had envisaged, more streamlined and austere in appearance, in order for it efficiently to carry the sheer volume of traffic anticipated for Europe's greatest city. On his visits to witness the construction's progress over the next five years, Hitler grew dissatisfied at those amendments, vociferously berating the architects and the Gauleiter of Linz, August Eigrüber; finally, he accepted the merits of the more functional design and chose not to overrule the architects, nor to slaughter them for their treachery, as Stalin would have done. But in photographs of Hitler on his final visit to the bridge, on its completion in 1943, he appears disgruntled and grim-faced, one hand pressed down on the granite parapet, gazing to the west as though startled, towards the Freidberg. A number of full-scale plaster models of horse-mounted figures from the *Nibelungenlied* had been installed at each end of the bridge, both to celebrate its completion and to appease Hitler, as a demonstration of how the bridge would eventually appear within his reconfigured city, with those plaster figures then transformed into marble; but, soon after his departure, the provisional figures began to crack and disintegrate, and were jettisoned into the fast-flowing river below. At the approach of the invading American forces, two years later, at the end of the Second World War, the entire bridge was mined for detonation by German engineers, to impede those forces' progress; but no officer dared give the order for the destruction of Hitler's bridge, and, in any case, it had been constructed to such exacting standards that it would have required an immense explosion, of the intensity used for Stalin's statue in Prague, to successfully destroy it. The Americans entered Linz shortly after Hitler's death, crossing the undefended bridge from the north. For the next decade, the bridge marked the fractious frontier-line between the zones of Austria occupied by the Soviet and American powers, barbed-wired and lethal, before eventually settling into the modest task of connecting central Linz with the Urfahr suburb, its original name intact, its dimensions excessively vast in scale and capacity for the restrained commuter needs of that provincial city.

Even in its contemporary banality, cast into obsolescence from its status as the envisaged core of Hitler's grandiose "Führerstadt," its history emptying out into oblivion, that bridge still formed an enduring crack at Europe's heart, emanating its malediction. I stood at the exact point on the bridge's western side where Hitler had been photographed in his morose dismay, aware, by that point in the war, in 1943, that his city would never be built, that even the plans for his bridge, conceived and designed as a mystical endeavor, from a position of absolute power and authority, to last forever, in glory, had been downgraded and standardized.

25

From the western parapet of Hitler's bridge, I crossed the empty traffic lanes and tram-tracks to the far side, and entered the Ars Electronica digital center. After paying the admission fee, I was given a bar-coded sticker to attach to the back of my hand, allowing me to access all of the center's exhibits. I took the elevator to the top floor, and walked through the rooms of corporeal simulations, where the center's visitors were able to materialize ghost images of their own heads on plasma screens, by triggering three-dimensional scans of their facial muscles' involuntary or intentional movements; talking while being scanned produced a violent digital blur. The glass-faced southern side of the building overlooked the Nibelungenbrücke, and as I passed down from level to level, that bridge changed shape, initially poised in cold magnificence against the city, then progressively declining in grandeur as it came closer to my eyes, its cracked tarmac and cut-price execution visible, its form flattening out from splendor to the banality that had offended its original architect.

At the southern end of the center's second floor, an overhead annex had been constructed, where three or four earnest young technicians were ready to operate an experimental virtual-reality system that allowed one user at a time the opportunity to fly digitally over Europe. Alongside the vast window looking out over the Danube bridge, several high-powered computers had been attached to virtual-reality headsets; a number of gray-and-red flight suits in different sizes, each equipped with harnesses, lay ready for the center's visitors. I watched several fathers attempt to persuade their children to be hoisted up for flight, but after inspecting the equipment closely, the children backed away with alarmed faces. I read the text stenciled on the wall beside the exhibit, which was sponsored by (and named after) one of the salubrious, image-screened department stores located in the avenue that ran south from Hitler's bridge: "On the Cyberdeck, the new Humphrey is waiting to take you along on a flight through virtual worlds. The user is positioned in midair by pneumatic muscles and uses arm movements to maneuver as a force feedback system simulates the physical forces at work during flight. It's completely intuitive, though skill and practice are necessary to record a top time in a race through a course marked out in the virtual airspace of Europe." I turned away and passed through the other floors of the center, then returned to the Cyberdeck. It was still empty, the technicians looking restive alongside their underused equipment. One of them caught my eye imploringly. The expensive exhibit had taken several years to program and had only just been installed; those young technicians' jobs depended on the center's visitors taking a mandatory minimum number of daily digital flights.

I stepped into one of the flight suits, put on a virtual-reality headset that engulfed my vision, and was hoisted fifteen feet into midair by the technicians, harnessed around the chest and shoulders, and bound flexibly to the data collection points on the ceiling by cables attached to the headset and to pulse-registering bands around my wrists. The headset's earphones were playing an organ piece by Mussorgsky. At first, the intensity of the high-resolution pixels hurt my eyes and made me momentarily nauseous, but soon I was flying, my arms outspread, the directional data transmitted from my eye- and arm-movements sending me headlong through the sky of a digitally generated Europe, exhaustively replicated down to the last building. Although the system marked out a set course to be followed by its users, I immediately disregarded it. At first, I was flying over Linz itself, dropping almost to the tarmac of Hitler's bridge, before sweeping upwards in elation, far above the summit of the Freidberg. Then I headed east, following the Danube, over the heart of Europe. The exhibit had been designed as a "race" for its user, to be conducted in alliance or conflict between the body in movement and the speed of the eye; I found I could travel with almost limitless velocity by synchronizing the concentration of my digital vision and the muscle tension of my arms, though the effort required for that simultaneity soon began to grow painful, gradually forcing apart my aching body and my over-focused eyes. Within a few minutes, I was over Budapest, compulsively circling the digital city, its animation rendered so exactly, updated constantly by satellite data feeds, that I could see every detail of the liberation monuments, the pioneer railway, and the gesturing figures of Lenin and Comrade Ostapenko in the outlying Statue Park. Pivoting my eyes and outstretched arms, I then headed due north, flying over the quarry-indented forests and polluted cities of central Slovakia, across the Tatra Mountains and the border with Poland, until I reached Kraków.

I sped over the city's market square and castle hill, circled the vast steelworks on the eastern edge of the city, then began to turn west, towards Oświęcim. Abruptly, I heard a sharp crack within the virtual-reality headset, directly in front of my eyes, and began to lose height and direction, diverted from the course I had chosen. I was suddenly blown backwards, the pixels that composed Kraków rapidly breaking up, fragmenting into virulent blocks of color. The soundtrack cut off, and I could hear the urgent voices of the young technicians, anxiously trying to locate the source of the malfunction. No longer able to control my course, I started to plummet towards the river Wisła, on the city's southern edge, expelled from that flight over Europe. At the exact moment I hit the surface of the river, just to the southwest of the Powstańców Bridge, the headset flashed in fiery white-heat extinguishment, blinding my eyes, then snapped off into darkness. I could feel the technicians hoisting me back down to the steel floor of the Cyberdeck; they removed the headset and checked my vital signs, apologizing for the mishap, and blaming that digital crash on the caprices of the inadequately tested new equipment. I stood upright, vertiginous, staring straight ahead. For a few seconds, my jarred vision failed to adapt, and a haywire concoction of all of the digital cities of Europe layered itself over my eyes. Then that apparition mercifully faded, and, with profound relief, I saw Hitler's bridge cohere directly in front of me.

26

As soon as I had recovered my equilibrium, I decided to leave Linz and travel to Kraków, to witness the location on the surface of the river Wisła where my digital flight had crashed down. I could still feel the sensation of a definitive expulsion from the heart of Europe that I had experienced during that plummet, and that sensation could only be dispelled by annulling the digital with the presence of my body. As I crossed the Danube bridge for the last time, my arms ached with aftershock jolts from their attempt to synchronize in digital flight with my vision, and my retinas were still being stabbed by the last incandescent incisions of haywire white light. I checked out from Hitler's room at the Wolfinger Hotel, reluctant to leave behind its cluttered array of nineteenth-century ephemera, now too long-engrained to make way for the immediate corporate imperatives of the contemporary city. I took the tram down the avenue to the vast business complex which housed the city's railway station at its ground level; a dense network of newly built fast-food concessions marked the center of the site where Hitler had intended all of Europe's great art to be amassed in his "Führermuseum." Standing on the platform, I took from my pocket the crumpled map I had drawn in Prague, under the imperial dome of the Hlavni Station concourse, weeks earlier.

Up to now, by accident or design, I had followed exactly the itinerary of scrambled pencil lines that I had traced across it; but to track the course of my digital flight over Europe would stretch that fragile map far beyond breaking point, and I jammed it back into my pocket.

The journey to Kraków, covered in a few minutes while suspended in midair at the Ars Electronica center, took over a week to accomplish on the ground; in order exactly to follow the course of the Danube eastwards, and then head north over central Slovakia to the Polish frontier, I had to take the tortuous routes of local trains that stopped at every rural hamlet, transporting peasants and their protesting animals to market. The express-train lines diverged too far away from the Danube on the first stage of the journey, across Austria and Hungary, and no express lines existed at all through the mountainous regions of central Slovakia, where I rode on one-carriage, once-a-day trains that wound their way at leisure around the scarcely populated valleys, stopping for hours on end at stations still marked with their century-old imperial signage. I entered another time of Europe. It was a land from which many inhabitants had fled for the long journey to the nearest ports, Gdańsk and Trieste, in the final decades of the nineteenth century, to emigrate to the industrial cities of the United States; most of the remaining male population had then been corralled up and slaughtered in the First World War. Occasionally, the train would pass by a toxic chemical plant exhaling vermilion smoke, and the air inside the reeling carriage would fill with yellow dust and turn unbreathable. But for every lethally functioning chemical plant, the train passed ten or more that had been long abandoned, the twisted amalgams of pipes now rusted away and scattered in disarray over the scoured industrial terrain. The avenues of the isolated towns where

I spent the nights at threadbare station hotels were crowded with drunkenly wrestling men and with women yelling curses and wielding beer bottles in their frenzy.

Since no railway line traversed the Tatra mountain-range, on the border between Slovakia and Poland, I was compelled to detour eastwards through its foothills; I crossed the frontier and finally approached Kraków on an evening train from the southeast. Without entering the city, I left the train at the suburban Zabłocie station, close to the river Wisła, in the district to which Kraków's Jewish inhabitants had been consigned in 1941, fragments of the ghetto walls still surviving among the area's rundown tenements. Descending the station's concrete stairway in the growing darkness, I headed at first in the wrong direction for the Powstańców Bridge, still disorientated by the wrench in time between the sheer velocity of my digital flight and the excruciating slowness of the subsequent week's journey. A few unpaved, unsigned pathways fanned out from the station exit, and a derelict railway track looped by from the direction of the enamel-factory complexes alongside that station. I followed the broken-glass-strewn track, every sleeper carrying an intricately spraycanned graffiti inscription, but it soon grew too obstructed by undergrowth for me to continue, and I turned back, finally reaching a road junction identifiable from the last moments of my digital flight over the city. A few seconds later, I was standing on the Powstańców Bridge, searching for the point on the surface below at which my flight had ended; that surface was calm and unbroken, the river moving with slow ease. I crossed the bridge to the far bank, on the southern edge of the city's Kazimierz district, and descended the stairway to the path alongside the river, scanning the water for the precise location of my fall, and attempting to match my memory of that fall's malfunctioning pixelated image with the current contents of my eyes. Young inhabitants of Kazimierz were sitting together at intervals on the stone-constructed riverbank, embracing or in silence, drinking from bottles of beer in the cool evening air, their legs dangling above the water. One boy flung a just-emptied Okocim bottle far over the river, into its center; it hung for a moment, neck up, emanating ripples, exactly at my digital impact zone, then filled with river-water and sank down into darkness.

27

I sat down on the riverbank, my legs hanging high over the water like those of the other figures poised along that stone parapet. The lights on the Powstańców Bridge came on, and the ruined warehouses and industrial buildings on the Zabłocie side of the river began to fade into the darkness. Some of the young inhabitants of that riverbank melted away towards the bars of the Kazimierz district, others simply deepened into their night's drinking without moving. The stars came out in the cold black sky above Kraków.

I watched the point on the river's surface where my flight had impacted, until it vanished into the darkness. Until its disintegration, the last destination of that flight over the heart of Europe had been Oświęcim, to the west of Kraków, and the two concentration-camp cities on that town's edge that had marked the erasure of any conception of Europe as a valuable entity, within the span of the planet that carried it: those cities had formed the obliterating inverse of Hitler's plans for the magnificent, culturally supreme city of Linz. Both of Hitler's projects, the grandiose and the genocidal, had become voids on the face of Europe, impossible to reconstruct, represent or envision. The digital crash my journey had incurred at the Ars Electronica center had also canceled out the corporeal time and space that would have allowed that journey to encompass those concentration-camp cities, or to end there. I could take out a cellphone and access a digital variant of Auschwitz composed of satellite images of the sites, scan condensed histories and statistics, speed-read bullet-pointed details of tourist facilities; I could even take the train from Kraków to Oświęcim, sit for hours in the station concourse's café and watch the clientele eating microwaved frozen pizzas at molded-plastic benches, or cross to the dimly lit bar over the road and take a seat beside the young drinkers of that town, each determinedly gripping a bottle of Okocim like the one just thrown into the river before my eyes. But I could never reach those cities and their inhabitants, only imagine them, and their permanent absence from Europe.

28

I stayed by the Wisła riverbank until most of its inhabitants had disappeared, uprooted even from the most profound of alcohol stupors by the saturating layer of freezing air that rose up from the black water, gradually enveloping their bodies from their feet up to their heads. The temperature was soon far below zero and I had to wrench myself away from the site of my flight's crash, vulnerable to the lethal exposure that would result from a few more hours of my body's stasis at that site, and aware too that the expulsion that crash had entailed had left my body entirely without the screening protection of the digital, against the city. That sensation of expulsion I had experienced could not be expunged. All of the strategies of memory that the digital had seemed to provide, in accelerating my perception, and in allowing me – with pinpoint immediacy – to situate the seminal locations of Europe's ecstasies and calamities, within its cities, had misfired and been abruptly withdrawn at the moment of that fall. The digital was now ineffectual in my search for those locations; I was left only with my body and eyes to track down the unique image, if one ever existed at all, that engulfed and projected the infinity of Europe's memory, at its heart.

I walked west along a curve in the riverbank, round the southern perimeter of the Kazimierz district, until I could see the old city amassed on its hilltop above the river. I climbed up, fast, my breath freezing into constellations of ice droplets with each exhalation, those droplets hovering in the air for an instant, then disintegrating into rushing splinters as my face broke through them. I passed the castle and headed into the core of the city. The alleyways' buildings had already ground themselves deep into decrepitude, centuries ago, and kept themselves still pinioned upright in the face of the city only through the plague crosses and the monuments to massacre that had been positioned at regular intervals between them; the sole transformation those buildings' surfaces had undergone in five centuries had been that inflicted by the high-level acid-rain pollution blown over from the Nowa Huta steelworks on the city's eastern edge, adding a seething new carapace of ruination to those surfaces. The night was too cold for all but the most determined drinkers or ascetics, and the trams rattled by near-empty. I reached the old city's vast central square and headed for the only café still open, the Noworolski, at the southwestern end of the colonnaded arcade that traversed the square's space. A few entrenched old men still sat in red-velvet chairs in the long succession of silent gilt rooms, reading newspapers and consulting account-books. The steaming radiators were working at full tilt to heat the rooms. It was in that café, then only a few decades old, that Lenin had spent most of the years 1912–14, at a corner table in the final room, in exiled isolation, writing polemics and methodically planning the revolutionary acts that would help send the remainder of the twentieth century into its free fall of intensive slaughter and utopian obsession, the debris spilling capriciously from that century into the next; Stalin briefly joined him in Kraków at the end of 1912. Lenin had arrived secretly in the city on June 22, 1912, on a night train from Vienna, and stayed for over two years, occasionally withdrawing into the anonymous international spa resorts of the Tatra Mountains, to avoid suspicion; he eventually left Kraków for Switzerland on August 20, 1914. I took his table in the Noworolski café, and a waiter delivered a minuscule cup of black coffee to its indented wooden surface. It was already well beyond the café's closing time, and the old men gradually dispersed, buttoning their greatcoats against the cold; even the waiters were leaving. I was the last figure remaining in the café on that freezing winter's night.

Eventually, I left Lenin's table and walked outside to the center of the square's immense, emptied space: all around, the cafés, hotels, and nightclubs were shuttered-up for the night, and there was nowhere left to go, nowhere to escape to or from. It was after two in the morning, and the entire city had decelerated to immobility. The multiple impacts of time upon the city appeared momentarily dispelled, rarefied now to the point that only the fragile noise of human cries in the far distance, and the faint resonance of my heartbeat right there in that silence, sustained that city's thin-air existence.

29

In order to maintain body heat, I decided to take the long road
on foot out to the Nowa Huta steelworks, on the city's eastern
periphery. The exact center of the square formed the optimum
point from which to track the sparse sonic and corporeal traces
of the city at the dead of night, but remaining on that spot
would leave me terminally rooted to that city, in iced sclerosis,
by dawn. I headed east, through the blackened-stone underpass
beneath the imperial edifice of the main railway station, and
along the hoarding-bordered avenue that led upwards out of
the city. As I ascended the higher ground, the vast industrial
panoramas of the eastern suburbs began to open up before me,
each satellite complex of furnaces and factories studded with
chimneys, the air directly above them glowing from the residue
of the previous day's emissions; in that sky, the stars were still
out. After a while, I abandoned the avenue and instead followed
the line of the Nowa Huta tram-track, its service suspended
for only three or four hours during the night; the track left the
avenue behind and cut directly through wooded parkland,
and I passed by the palatial psychiatric hospital of eastern
Kraków, the lights out for the night, the inmates' screaming
still full-throttle. The closer I came to Nowa Huta, the more the
buildings appeared intensively marked by acid-rain corrosion,
great crusts of chemical residue configuring the resilient sides
of the century-old tenements, and sprawling virulently over
the graffiti'd facades of the shoddy 1960s concrete-block towers,
the fluorescent spraycanned inscriptions enmeshed with those
brittle, noxious scars. I could see the Nowa Huta chimneys
in the distance, their soaring forms barring the eastern sky.
Those chimneys had now been filtered; no longer able to inflict
premium-grade toxic damage on the internal organs of the

city's inhabitants and on its buildings' facades, as they had done for over five decades, they still formed an ominous presence at that city's edge.

By the time the tram-track reached Nowa Huta's Plac Centralny, at the foot of the avenue that led up to the main gates of the steelworks complex, my body temperature had been restored by the non-stop walk. On three sides of that square, robust marble apartment blocks had been constructed in the final years of Stalin's life, in the style that had extended right across eastern Europe, from Moscow to Berlin's Stalin-Allee and Prague's Hotel International; the planned southern side of the square had been unaccountably left unbuilt, and from the vantage-point of that void, the city's industrial zones lay spread out, all the way down to the banks of the Wisła and the Powstańców Bridge. A statue of Lenin had been erected in the square in the early 1950s, and his name accorded to the steelworks, to commemorate his revolutionary machinations of forty years earlier, conducted down below at his table in the city's Noworolski café; but the Nowa Huta steelworks had formed one of the pivotal sites of Polish anti-communist workers' unrest in the 1970s and 1980s, and the statue had vanished, along with the name of Lenin. The bannered advertising-hoardings clamped to the apartment blocks' rooftops now looked down on an empty square of beerbottle-strewn grass and cracked concrete benches. Avenues of identical blocks radiated out from the Plac Centralny in a rigorous star shape, originally constructed to house the steelworkers and their pioneer children; I could see the first lights now going on in the windows of those blocks, as I headed up the Solidarności avenue to the Nowa Huta gateway.

The coldest moment of the night coincided with my arrival at the gateway. For the first time since leaving Kraków's central square, three hours earlier, I came to a halt. It was still dark, and the immense sign carrying the illuminated name of the steelworks rose high above me, the individual letters seemingly suspended in midair over the armatures of two inverted pyramids; on either side, enormous administration blocks with castellated summits guarded the entrance to that city of fire. Steelworkers were beginning to arrive on the morning's first trams for the 5.30 a.m. shift, and I followed them inside, into the terrain of innumerable chimney-surmounted furnaces and industrial warehouses that stretched for miles in every direction, rapidly engulfing those figures. The noise of the buildings was beginning to roar into momentum, unstoppable until the next fall of night. I stopped dead, then abruptly turned back, against the direction of the growing mass of bodies, and left that contaminated city.

30

At the Nowa Huta terminus, across the avenue from the steelworks' gateway, great floods of workers were shouldering themselves out of the arriving trams, heading determinedly inside that gateway. It was still dark, freezing cold, with pulses of sleet beginning to fall. It took some time for the first tram of the morning to clank into life and head back down into the city; there were no other passengers. All along the Solidarności avenue, I watched trams heading in the opposite direction, thirty seconds apart, saturated with bodies, the interiors of their windows liquid with steaming corporeal heat. The chemical-seared buildings I had passed on foot on my way up to Nowa Huta now appeared in reverse, intermittently visible through the growing torrents of sleet, as though their forms had been imprinted into deteriorated film images that were now speeding by in accelerated rewind. I left the tram outside the main railway station; the unkempt imperial hotels around the station's plaza were turning off their neon signs for the night – Europejski Hotel, Wczoraj Hotel – as the darkness shaded marginally into dawn. I walked through the deserted, wood-paneled ticket-hallways to check the departure board for the first trains of the day. A slow train of two ancient carriages was about to leave for the industrial city of Ostrava, over the Czech border, where my airplane flight, marooned in suspension over Europe, had momentarily come aground, at the beginning of my journey. I took a seat in the overheated second carriage, exhausted after the night's walk, and fell asleep.

An hour later, I woke with a start as the train made its first stop. On one side of the carriage, through the ragged wall of sleet, I could see vast marshaling yards and long lines of cargo wagons, unused for decades. On the other side, I caught sight of the station's name, the old enameled sign barely able to project its contents through streaks of red rust: Oświęcim. I stood up, dazed, and descended to the platform as the train moved slowly on towards Ostrava. Inside the high-ceilinged station concourse, a scattering of alcoholic residents, strangely euphoric and garrulous, gripped bottles of rowan-flavored vodka. I walked over to the exit: the sleet was pounding down, turning the plaza's surface to slate-gray mud. Across the road, the town's bar was still shuttered; behind it, a few streets of mundane housing blocks gradually faded into their vanishing point within the sodden, opaque air. Away to the left, the spinning aluminum planet that surmounted the tower of the communist-era Glob Hotel was just visible. In the 1920s and 1930s, that town had been notorious for the vivacity and uproar of its dancehalls, where celebrations were held every Saturday night to mark the eighteenth birthdays of peasant women from the surrounding villages; Oświęcim was known throughout the rural, poverty-stricken Małopolska region as the "town of flowers," from the masses of irises and lilies brought to those celebrations, and left behind, on Sunday mornings, in its streets. Young men from the region often emigrated to work in the acid and horse-glue factories on the peripheries of Paris, in the northern suburb of Aubervilliers, where the work was so hard and dangerous that few local workers could be found to undertake it. But the town of Oświęcim sustained its negligible presence on the planet, stranded far from the oceans, but embedded by its buildings' foundations into the earth's surface. Then, five or six years flashed by and the town became transformed, compressed to asphyxiation by the concentration-camp cities erected and then destroyed or abandoned on its edges; that town was then reduced into the form of an airless transit zone for journeys into the traces of Europe's systemic massacres.

I took a seat in the station concourse's café and ordered a coffee. From my table, I could see the station's entrance and the plaza outside. Then, the time deepened. Occasionally, passengers would enter the café and buy provisions at the counter that ran along one side of it. Otherwise, the young waitress sat motionless on a plastic chair, looking into space. The concourse's alcoholic residents sprawled out on the wooden benches and lost consciousness. Every few hours, a train entered and left the station. Every few hours, I ordered another coffee. The day went by; the fall of sleet diminished in mid-afternoon, and the light began to fail again; the town outside disappeared.

Oświęcim had been the planned final destination of the digital flight over the heart of Europe I had undertaken in Linz's

Ars Electronica center. When my flight crashed prematurely into the river Wisła, I believed that impact had canceled forever the possibility of my body being able to complete the journey, and that the vital core of Europe's wound had been barriered to me. But the power of the digital had evanesced at the moment when I located and inhabited that crash site, on the southern edge of Kraków, and I saw now that it was only my own body that carried the failure to finally complete that journey. My body and Europe could not mesh, or be reconciled, but could only grate away indefinitely, as though eye to eye, at one another's surface. And so, that journey could not end, but only persist, in its annulled search for a revelation of Europe; I could hear, far above my head, the station's amplification system urgently announcing the arrival of the night train for Vienna, and I ran for the platform.

31

By the time the night train reached Vienna at dawn the following morning, traveling in the reverse direction to Lenin's journey to Kraków of June 1912, any recollection I still held of my digital fall had evanesced, hidden forever now below the freezing surface of the river Wisła, or lost somewhere in the technology-free unconsciousness of the Oświęcim station's alcoholic vagrants, though the traces of Europe's massacres and maledictions continued to surround me, inhabiting an aching peripheral vision, as I settled into endless nights of walking through the city. I took a room in an outbuilding of the Habsburg palace, in the silent center of that city, determined to remain in Vienna for the rest of the winter, and to allow the image that carried the infinity of Europe's memory, that I had been searching out, without success, in determined compulsion, on my journey through Europe's heart, to arrive now without warning, of its own volition, if it existed at all. I would do nothing but open my eyes in the city.

By day, I looked through collections of photographs and documentary film-stills of the firebombed city of Vienna from the last period of the Second World War and the subsequent decade; although that city had not been erased as comprehensively as other cities of central Europe, and its population had avoided mass incineration, its overhaul by fire had scrambled its prewar alignments and created its contemporary form. The greatest intensity of devastation had taken place as the Soviet forces finally fought their way into the city in April 1945, blowing apart and igniting its cathedral with artillery shells as they advanced; the sky had glowed scarlet over the city every night. The Soviet soldiers killed in that assault had been buried together in the cemetery on the city's edge. Many destroyed buildings in the inner city had remained as heaped rubble for the subsequent decade of occupation, the city's population projected outwards to the expanding suburbs, or simply habituating themselves to inhabiting zones of urban wreckage; when large-scale reconstruction became possible, the city's pitted terrain of flattened apartment houses rapidly metamorphosed into streamlined office blocks and department stores. In those photographs and film-stills, the human bodies traversing the ruined city form slight, fragile residues within vastly amassed debris.

Each night, I tracked my way through the inner-city configuration, blowing out iced exhalations in the silent air, from the illuminated Graben avenue into the meshed alleyways to the east, following the fracture lines and puncture points from those photographic images of the dislocated city. In the darkness, whatever wounding that city had undergone had been sutured over, its presence now tangible only in abrupt dead-ends and openings of over-vast and empty squares. Up above, through the lit windows of apartment houses, I could see successions of lushly chandelier'd rooms, those spaces blurred from time to time with the nocturnal movements of their occupants. As I walked eastwards, bursts of young nightclubbers exited cellars in momentary cacophonies, trailing disintegrating phantoms of body heat behind them in the chilled air, before evanescing into the darkness. The alleyways' emptiness grew profound as the night went on, broken only by the occasional figures of wakeful old men, shrunken into greatcoats, moving restlessly in the cold, too abrasively scoured by memory or pain to disappear into the city's oblivion, or to grow still. Towards dawn, I would leave behind the multiple convolutions of the inner city, and head south over the Kärtner ring road towards the Südbahnhof railway station, past the granite memorial column that lauded the Soviet forces who had seized control of the city in the final battles of 1945. All of the city's railway stations had been obliterated during that conflict, then reconstructed over the subsequent decade; the Südbahnhof's rawly exposed interior space opened out into levels of resilient gray ferro-concrete, its escalators ascending to the platforms, where the early-morning trains were preparing to leave for Bratislava and Trieste. On the station's concourse, crossed at speed by the departing passengers and rigorously scanned by surveillance cameras, no excess gestures were enacted, and no superfluous human figures could be encompassed: time was exhaustively stripped to the bone, even before the day had begun. Deflected from that space, I would return to the street, to walk the final stretch back to my room in the first light.

32

After a month of night-long walking through the inner-city network of alleyways and squares, intent on interrogating every askew flaw and void in their form, and layering the contents of my eyes over the photographic traces of the city's destruction, I had got nowhere. My eyes had grown too intimately complicit with the evidence of ruination during my journey through Europe, and I could now discern nothing at all at ground level. Only the disjointed fragments of naked human bodies glimpsed through the windows of high-ceilinged apartments, in the dead of night, or the multiply lined faces of the insomniac old men I passed in the Judenplatz, deeply swathed within the collars of half-century-old overcoats, still focused my eyes upon the city. The worst of the winter was now already over, and I could feel the delicate prospect that had driven my journey, of seizing a revelation or cancellation of Europe, slipping away between my fingers, to fall and shatter on the still-frozen ground. One night, instead of entering again the inner city's morass of alleyways, I decided to climb to the top of the Leopoldsberg hill, rising directly to the north of Vienna, in order to feel the city closer to my body, to allow my eyes to pinpoint any vital flaw in its surface that might lead directly down, or up, into its heart.

From the tram terminus at the foot of the Leopoldsberg, I ascended the twisting hill-road alongside vineyard terraces; soon, the houses and streetlights gave out and I was climbing through the darkness of the forest. Towards the peak of the hill, the road gave out too, and I followed a path through the trees towards the church that marked the hill's summit. I could hear animals constantly moving in the undergrowth, exhaling in exertion; towards the summit, the urgent but barely audible noise of two people having sex, in the isolation of that night

– two men, or a man and a woman, or two women: it was impossible to say – echoed under the forest canopy, bleeding into the other sounds of the night, shifting erratically in register into a sequence of raw cries, then suddenly plunging into silence. I started to wonder if I had been wrong to search only for an image of Europe's memory, on my journey: far more likely, it was instead a sound – or the sensorial immediacy of that memory, transmitted through sound, and binding city to city and body to body – that could conceivably be held. An image could never be held, without transforming beyond recognition, from second to second, and slipping away; nor did an image have the power to project the enduring substance of a wound or an ecstasy, or of a memory, of Europe – an image could only jar uselessly, as a momentary irritant within the membranes of the eye.

It was from the vantage-point of the Leopoldsberg's peak, above the forest line, that the Polish king Jan Sobieski had gauged the exact strength and distribution of the Turkish army that had encircled and lain siege to Vienna, in 1683, before receiving a papal blessing and descending the hill, headlong, with his forces, to decimate that army and liberate the city, earning for himself the epithet of the "savior of Europe," by halting the westward advance of the Ottoman Empire; the church on the hill's summit had been constructed to commemorate that ocular triumph. A low-walled terrace of slate flagstones had been built around the now-decrepit building, vulnerable for centuries to battering east winds from the Carpathian Mountains; a few figures were scattered over that terrace's edge, looking down at the illuminated city below, and I joined them. From that height, every last element of the city was visible, seamed north to south by the Danube, the suburbs and corporate satellites gesturing directly outwards in lines to the east and west, the dense mass of the inner-city core fused into lucid silver amalgams, its form no longer incoherent or fractured, its marks and levels of damage dissolved away into its incandescent surface; the entire configuration of that city appeared, like that of Linz, as a skeletal human body, now abruptly pushed backwards to the ground, forcibly spread-eagled and exposed. A few digital image-screens were obstinately transmitting through the night, from the roofs of buildings along the eastern bank of the Danube, glowing upwards into the sky in scarlet and white light; their pixels' content and corporate affiliation could not fully reach my eyes at that distance, the simultaneity and integrity of their projection and perception now broken, and I could catch only the faintest residue of eroded lettering or malformed bodies, exuded by those screens.

I let the flawless city gradually permeate my eyes until there was nothing left to be seen: no city, no images. After a few hours, its illumination began to fade away, the image-screens were extinguished, and the buildings' surfaces emerged, their constellations irregular and flawed, once again, to my eyes, with the first daylight. The terrace had emptied. I left the Leopoldsberg by the sheer pathway that ran directly downwards from the summit to the western bank of the Danube. That pathway could only be descended, at speed; its gradient was too precipitous to be ascended, except by the over-agile National Socialist pioneers who had constructed it at the end of the 1930s. Only the pathway's concertina'd switchbacks impeded that vertiginous fall, my feet struggling to maintain balance, moving faster and faster, until that pathway exhausted itself at ground level beside the Danube.

33

I walked northwards along the bank of the Danube, away from the city, until the north face of the Leopoldsberg had blocked that city's presence away from my eyes and ears. After an hour, I reached the riverside wooden-hut settlements of Klosterneuberg; great chunks of lurid mud, dead animals, and a thousand kinds of debris were racing just below the river's ochre surface. A few figures emerged from the nearby huts and stood attentively alongside me in the dawn light, as though witnessing an exceptional spectacle rather than a permanent component of their lives. The river was noisier and far wider here than in Budapest or Linz, churning its detritus in turbulent pulses and splinterings; at the time of Jan Sobieski's victory over the Turkish army, it had formed several distinct branches at this point, with oxbow lakes stranded like severed arms in the surrounding terrain. Although its course had since been channeled, and it traversed the center of Vienna in the straitened form of a subsidiary canal, that river still seethed with volatile power through the cities at the heart of Europe, poisoned and deformed by them, bridged by dictators, but able still to nonchalantly swamp those cities at will, until it expanded still further, eastwards, into a swollen artery for the criminal smuggling of oil and prostitutes, traversing Romania and finally disintegrating into the Black Sea deltas to the north of Constanța.

The uproar of that river made my head swim after a few hours beside it, and the cities I had traveled through seemed to whip into convulsive flux around me, spinning in a chaotic vortex of interpenetrated human bodies and sites of massacre; I started to feel that I would never pinpoint or isolate any space or image of Europe. In order to stop time, for a moment of respite,

I decided to visit the field of graves of the Soviet soldiers killed during their assault on the city in 1945, in the vast cemetery on the far side of Vienna. I took the train from Klosterneuberg back into the city, then the underground train through the industrial southeastern suburbs; the signs of the journey soon turned ominous, as the train passed through desolate stations named "Gasometer" and "Slaughterhouse-Street," but by the final stage, by tram to the gates of that immense city of the dead, the morning had been illuminated by late-winter sun, the gaps between the suburban factories and apartment blocks opening out into panoramas towards the empty border plains of Hungary and Slovakia.

I found the Soviet soldiers hidden behind the domed church in the center of the cemetery. It was silent there, under the trees; the fall of leaves from the previous autumn had never been cleared, and the field of graves was shin deep in brittle foliage that cracked like weapons-fire as I walked along the lines of headstones. Below the soldiers' names, almost all of the graves held the same date – April 11, 1945 – that of the severest fighting, as the Soviet forces entered Vienna. Their surviving comrades, in triumph, had then systematically abused and robbed the city's inhabitants, for days on end, in cruel elation, as in every destination-point city of the Soviet forces. Although each of the gravestones' surfaces was imprinted with a red star, the enamel-coated photographs of the soldiers had been distributed erratically, many surfaces left without images; the photographs, taken in studios in Kiev or Kharkov, showed young faces, male and female, seized at the instant of the film's exposure, wryly smiling or exuding determination. In most cases, their uniforms appeared brand new, and the photographs must have been taken soon after their enlistment, at Hitler's invasion of the Soviet Union in 1941, before that cataclysmic journey was unleashed, east to west across the blackened face of Europe, submerging millions of lives on the way, until the simultaneous instant of their own deaths, on that city's contested periphery, at the very last moment of the conflict.

I took the long path towards the northwestern cemetery gate, to begin walking back into the city. Along the way, I passed lines of Jewish gravestones from the earlier decades of the twentieth century, their surfaces embedded with multiple scars: struck with machine-gun bullet-impacts and hammer-blows soon after the National Socialist annexation of Austria in 1938, damaged still further, seven years later, by blasts of artillery fire during the Soviet forces' incursion into the city, via that cemetery, and then suspended indefinitely in time with those violent traces as a permanent part of their surfaces. Many thousands of broken gravestone fragments had been placed in haphazard piles on the ground, half-named, or less, inextricably entangled with one another, and irrecoverable.

34

After nearly two months of tracking the inner-city network of alleyways, through night-long walks within its oblique systems and closed-down dead-ends, I grew convinced that there was no engulfing image of Europe's heart to be found in that city. From that morning in the cemetery when I had scanned the identical, simultaneous dates on the gravestones of the Soviet soldiers, synchronized to one instant of death, I found I could perceive less and less of the time of the city. My vision concentrated down into the exact moments at which it registered a blurred content of graffiti'd wall-surface, or a jolted shard of a human face, and I became immediately enmeshed in those moments and their sensorial impacts; but I received no memory, no image, from those glancing contacts. I was fortressed away from Europe within that city. The last of the winter snowfalls was beginning to melt in the gaps between buildings, and the first purple flowers of the spring emerged from the ground in the Burggarten. I knew I would soon have to abandon my journey. But that city remained adhesive, enclosing me within it. One dawn, arriving on the deserted concourse of the Südbahnhof station, I made an aberrant escape movement; on the upper platform level, side-by-side, the early-morning trains for Bratislava and Trieste were revving up for departure. All through that winter in the landlocked heart of Europe, I had seen nothing of the ocean, and I was now seized by the desire to reach it. Pulled out of joint by that desire, the corporeal focus of my mapped journey abruptly shattered, and I boarded the final carriage of the Trieste train just as its doors began to close.

But I could not escape Vienna: Trieste had been constructed in the eighteenth century to form a grandiose port-annex to that city and its empire, the monumental apartment blocks and palatial civic buildings intended to mirror those of Vienna. Since the collapse of that empire at the end of the First World War, Trieste had been thrown into a long sequence of haywire maneuvers, poised at a tectonic collision point in Europe's twentieth-century nationalistic face-offs, repeatedly contested and then nonchalantly discarded, until it finally lapsed into near-dereliction, saved from depopulation only by its suburbs' substandard digital industries. It was late afternoon before the train from Vienna arrived in Trieste; from the low-slung marble railway station, I walked to the Piazza Oberdan and took the decrepit cable-tramway to the immense limestone plateau high up above the city, the Carso, its surface still intricately scarred with the complex of combat trenches dug into it during the First World War. From that isolated summit, on the border between Slovenia and Italy, with the wind blowing in from every direction, I could see the Habsburg-built avenues of the city below, overcast at street level, the main squares opening directly to the sea: a scaled-down, oceanic variant of Vienna, its industrial-estate outskirts trailing haphazardly away to the east, along the spit of land between the mountains and the Adriatic.

By the time the tramway-carriage had lurched and squealed its way back down to ground level in the Piazza Oberdan, the city was darkening. I entered the imperial zone; only its regular arrangement, constructed in a grid of parallel apartment block avenues and studded with geometric squares, distanced it from the more convoluted, knocked-awry arteries of Vienna. A splinter from the heart of Europe had come unstuck here, propelled as an urban fragment to its far peripheries, taking the form of that one-square-mile grid by the ocean, positioned at a volatile intersection of Europe's fissurations, and as opaque and closed to revelation as the city to the north on which it was modeled. By the time I crossed the boulevard at the water's edge to reach the ocean, the city behind me had been illuminated for the evening, its inhabitants emerging from their dilapidated apartment blocks, to traverse the seafront squares in elegant leisure. I walked out along the narrow stone pier that led into the ocean; scatterings of young drinkers were seated on either side of that pier, their legs dangling over the polluted water, many of them embracing between alcohol gulps, like the figures beside the Powstańców river bridge in Kraków. Out to sea, emptied tankers were heading away from the city into the Adriatic shipping lanes, the crackling words of their navigators' radio transmissions just audible above the low noise of the waves; in the far distance, I could see the glow of light over the island city of Venice.

I walked back towards the railway station, where the same train on which I had traveled from Vienna that dawn was now preparing to make the reverse journey, departing at midnight to head northwards through the Friuli plain and back through the mountains into Austria. I left behind the city's imperial avenues and entered the terrain of disused warehouses alongside the station's marshaling yards; the vast metal facades of the warehouses had grown imprinted over decades with seasalt-enhanced rust corrosion, those expanses forming entire worlds of intricately layered and entangled damage, wildly seething and tainted, the surfaces virulently eaten away to their core, like authentic maps of Europe.

35

The train from Trieste passed through the plains and mountains and arrived back at the Südbahnhof station the following dawn. Everything was exactly as it had been, twenty-four hours earlier; that train was now being prepared for its imminent return to the south, while the Bratislava express alongside was gathering up its scarce passengers for its one-hour journey eastwards. I descended the elevator into the pristine concrete concourse of the station, ready to walk back through the Belvedere gardens to my room in the inner city. But as I stepped out into the street, I realized that no re-entry was now possible, back into that city, if any chance still survived, for my eyes finally to seize the image of Europe that I had been searching for; my journey had to be driven onwards. I returned to the platform level to catch the Bratislava express, but it had just pulled out. The railwayman who had signaled it away told me there was now no direct train until mid-afternoon, but, if I wished, I could take the circuitous route, via the local train to the village of Marchegg, on the border with Slovakia, and pick up a train to Bratislava from there. I stood on a side platform for an hour, waiting for that local train to pull in. During that hour, young women from every eastern European country began to appear, fifteen or twenty in all, each approaching me to ask, in cracked German, if this was the right place for the train to Bratislava. The women wore high-heeled boots, leather coats, multilayered make-up, and smoked rapid-fire cigarettes. They wanted simply to hear the word "yes," but I tried to explain that it was necessary to change trains in Marchegg, and those unknown words made their fragile faces convulse in exasperation. Although alone, they began to speak tentatively to one another in an unwillingly shared language, English, in successive monologues of wry lamentation, and I understood they were women returning from the great sex industries of western Europe, channeled back to Vienna in order to cross to Bratislava, where the weekly night expresses departed for their home cities in the east, to Kishinev and Lvov and Mukachevo. Some of them had just left their friends or associates at the international bus station beside the Südbahnhof, from where three-night-long economy journeys to those same cities, and those located still farther to the southeast, undertaken in battered coaches with ripped pvc seating and amphetamine-propelled drivers, could be attempted; but to return home by train was the mark of an elite.

The local train to Marchegg finally spluttered into the Südbahnhof, picked up its passengers and immediately set out again. In that one carriage, there were only the sex-industry women, each occupying a separate row of seats, tenaciously gripping the bags that held their last six months' earnings, together with one or two glowering peasants, and a scattering of grim-faced inhabitants of the near-moribund nihilistic sex communes that had sprung up in the early 1970s, in the isolated farmlands to the east of Vienna, and still subsisted, their surviving participants now exhausted by decades of relentless sexual activity. I had no idea exactly where Marchegg was located, but the train seemed to be heading northeast-wards. Once we were moving through the featureless open fields, dense sheets of early-morning rain began to come down, pummeling the roof and windows of the carriage, and the world outside vanished; a silence had fallen between the women, their empathy drained, and each sat in solitude. After an hour or so, the train pulled into the unsigned Marchegg station, and the driver switched off its engine to indicate that it had reached its destination. I could see that the women were baffled why we had stopped in the middle of nowhere, in a station that lacked a city, or a shelter, or even a platform; the village of Marchegg was nowhere in sight, if it existed at all. But the driver brusquely gestured them out, and they jumped down into the mud beside the railway track, their high heels impaling themselves in the semi-liquidized red earth. The peasants and nihilists disappeared into the rain, and the empty train set off back for Vienna; there was no indication of when a train from Bratislava would come to collect us. The rain was still pounding down, and the sodden sex-industry women stood in a jagged line beside the railway track, in resigned bewilderment, their ankles slowly sinking into the mud. We were stranded only a few miles from Bratislava. Through the breaks between the squalls of rain, I caught sight of the chemical factories on that city's periphery, the chimneys pumping out vertical bursts of vermilion flame. The hours went by and, for a moment, exhausted by the previous night's journey and beginning now to hallucinate from the exertion of standing upright, indefinitely, in that abysmal crossing zone, I imagined myself in Naples, the legendary terminal point of all sexual grand-tours of Europe, with the city's infernal fields of fire, expelling white-hot columns of toxic volcanic gas, all around. But then I snapped back into lucid consciousness, as a still more decrepit one-carriage train abruptly appeared out of the rain from Bratislava, as an act of mercy.

Once we were moving again, passing through the outlying factories and housing-block satellites and into the city, the sex-industry women brightened, and they began to wring out their lavish rain-soaked hair onto the floor and re-apply their make-up, offering caustic encouragement to one another. The Slovakian train guard asked to see their tickets, but they simply clicked their tongues and waved him away with dismissive derision. We were out of the void.

36

After twenty minutes of jolting its way through the peripheries of Bratislava, the train reached the central station, the empty platforms spread out under the final spur of the Carpathian Mountains; the sex-industry women filed out of the carriage and headed for the station café, to efface the span of time until their night trains left for the east, twelve hours later. The concourse was filled to capacity with gesturing groups of men, though nobody appeared to be intending to travel anywhere. I threaded my way through those bodies to enter the city. At first, from the station exit, all I could see were tangled road junctions, flyovers, and underpasses, traversed at full tilt by disintegrating cars and jam-packed buses. Finally, I located a subterranean pathway that took me beneath the twisted system of roads, the vehicles' tires pounding relentlessly at the thin membrane of fissured concrete over my head; that tunnel led all the way to the Nový Most bridge. I re-emerged into the gasoline-saturated air beside the plague column that now marked the boundary of Bratislava's inner-city core, its swathe of nineteenth-century avenues abruptly compressed by demolition, during the early 1970s, in order to make way for a sprawling bus station, constructed within a wasteland at the bridge's eastern limit. I continued along that bridge's pedestrian walkway, ten feet below the dense traffic lanes. On one side, to the south, I could see the expanse of the Danube, fast-moving and near-black with silt; at the other side, the walkway's wall formed an intensive screen of spraycanned and markerpen-inscribed graffiti, stretching from end to end of the bridge, worked and endlessly reworked over a decade or more into an immense compendium of sexual obsession, political confrontation, hatred, satanic mania, banality, gratuitous exclamation: the entire sensorium of that city's teenaged population, skinned alive and then exposed in raw denudation over that oblivious surface.

At the western limit of the Nový Most bridge, an elevator shaft ascended hundreds of feet upwards, at an askew angle, through an aluminum-encased tower. At first, I thought it must be long-disused, but then I caught sight of an old man, eighty or more years of age, dressed in a dark polyester suit, ready to operate the elevator's controls and accompany anyone willing to pay a low-value coin to the summit. The elevator jarred into action along its oblique trajectory. I looked into the old man's eyes; around them, the pallid skin carried profound furrows.

Sensing my unease, he began to narrate the journey for me, in shards of German learned after the invasion of 1939: he had held the position of elevator-operator ever since that bridge had been built, in the 1970s, and his wife sold postcards of the bridge in the café at the tower's summit. Holding my shoulder, he gestured with his hands through the glass windows of the elevator towards a hill above the inner city: up there was the Soviet war monument, and just below, the house where the hero of the Prague Spring, Alexander Dubček, had lived. Gently swiveling my line of vision into the opposite direction, as the ascent reached its midpoint and the city began to open out, he showed me the immense Petrzalka concrete-block housing estate, its identical white-and-red towers extending almost infinitely southwestwards: built in record time, again in the 1970s, the most vast housing estate in Europe, its population over a million strong. The surviving city appeared to have been constructed in two short bursts, in the 1830s and 1970s, with everything in between cursorily razed to the ground; all that had been appended since was a halfhearted scattering of corporate towers, and a colossal shopping complex, the "Europa-Center," located directly below that elevator tower, its array of digital advertising-screens illegible at that vertical angle.

The elevator door opened, and I could see concentrated streams of light reflected from the Danube, glittering and ricocheting around that space of engulfing windows, the deserted café-tables forming a revolving circle far above the city. Unable to face that assault of light, my eyes' resistance too depleted by the incessant journeys of the previous nights, I asked the operator to take me straight back down again; benignly, he cracked a smile and returned me to ground level, and I headed back along the bridge's walkway, into the inner city. I tried to find a place to sleep, but the colonnaded palace-hotel on the Danube's eastern bank was surrounded by black-clad armed guards, glaring in hostility, like those patrolling the liberation memorial in Budapest; the President of the United States of America was staying at that hotel, having delivered an open-air speech on the previous day, in which he had promised the ecstatic inhabitants of Bratislava that his country would help Slovakia in building up its military power. I kept on walking until I found an empty, twenty-story hotel from the communist era, where the rooms were still assigned to guests in a rigorously stratified order, working downwards from the far-end room of the top story, and I took that room.

37

At dawn the following morning, I began to follow the gestures over the city that had been enacted by the hands of the aged elevator-operator, during our twenty-second ascent to the summit of the Nový Most bridge; the fluid movements of those liver-spotted hands and gnarled fingers, oscillating with infinite suppleness from one side of the city to the other, in order to locate the determining points within its surface, were now compacted in my mind with the impenetrable network of incised and overdrawn lines of age on his face. The presence of that intricate corporeal network had been intimately close to my own face, in that constricted space, and formed the precursor to another map of Europe, obsolescent but more vital than ever, that could supplant or annul the one I still held crumpled in my pocket. I felt that I could have listened to his disjointed narrative of that despoiled city indefinitely, cross-referencing his words with the furrowed facial lines held a few inches from my eyes. But that fixed elevator-transit through space had brought the narrative to a close after just a few moments, and I was left only with the memory of that extraordinary face, and with the few gestured indicators of the city which his hands had revealed to me.

I crossed the inner-city avenues, still deserted at that hour, and began to climb the narrow road up the Slavín hill, to the Soviet war monument. That route, almost as precipitous as the Leopoldsberg's pioneer-constructed path, veered wildly from side to side as it ascended, bordered by the overgrown gardens of decrepit mid-nineteenth-century and Bauhaus-era villas, many of them evidently abandoned for decades, the villas' walls still streaked by bursts of machine-gun fire from the fierce fighting over that hill at the end of the Second World War; other villas, nearer the hilltop, had been restored, their facades replaced with great plate-glass screens, the driveways packed with expensive Swedish cars. On the hill's plateau, far above the city, a fifty-meter-high granite obelisk, surmounted by the colossal figure of a swastika-crushing, flag-wielding Soviet soldier, had been erected on the burial ground of the thousands of Ukrainian shock troops who had been killed in their assault on that city; like the soldiers in the Vienna cemetery, they had almost all died on the same day – April 4, 1945 – before the survivors regrouped and headed further west across the plain to Vienna, which they had entered exactly a week later. While the other Soviet war memorials across the cities of Europe had been constructed in the years directly following the end of the conflict, often using for their materials the lavish debris of National Socialist palaces, such as Hitler's Berlin Chancellery, the Bratislava monument, far vaster than the others, had been completed only in the early 1960s; the plans for its construction had been as grandiose as those for Stalin's statue in Prague, realizable on the punitive summit of that sheer hill only through a disciplined obsessionality in their executors' act of memory.

In the years since the communist era's end, the concentrated momentum that had created that memorial to the Soviet dead had transformed itself into a frozen oblivion that now enclosed that cryogenic site, isolated in thin air, high above the city and the central European plains; the memorial appeared to have been left in utter suspension, undamaged and un-relocated, and unvisited too. It lacked even the attentions of the young inhabitants of the Petrzalka housing blocks who had painstakingly graffiti'd every last surface of the Nový Most bridge walkways, but had clearly been deterred from also spraycanning that memorial by the too-exhausting ascent required to reach it. The friezes around the colonnaded base of the obelisk remained in flawless condition; in contrast to the earlier monuments, in other cities of central Europe, the rows of bronze-cast images stressed the technologies that had helped secure the Soviet victory, showing the embattled shock troops animatedly using field-telephones and other communications media. Those figures in combat were foregrounded against explicit representations of tortured Slovakian partisans, the lacerated women bare-breasted and open-mouthed in horror; defeated multitudes of blown apart or humiliated German soldiers appeared too, every figure rendered in glaring relief, as though their forms had been derived from strident fiction film images rather than the immediate memory of that conflict. Other, image-less bronze screens simply recorded dates and the names of cities, tracking the few days' span of the Soviet forces' movement westwards through Slovakia, a raw slice of slaughtered time, ending abruptly with the date of their arrival in Bratislava.

From the base of the memorial obelisk, with the figure of the Soviet soldier towering above me, I looked out northeastwards towards the accumulating spurs of the Carpathian mountain range, each mass of black rock growing in volume and height with their distance from the city. Directly below, the inner-city core was marooned within its carapace of entangled arterial ring roads, and over the Danube, I could see the innumerable housing blocks of the Petrzalka estate extending outwards, in rigid sequences of immense triangular shapes, from their apex at the western limit of the Nový Most bridge. I left the dead, hanging over the city in their silence, and started to descend.

38

Throughout my descent, the Petrzalka satellite city remained in sight, gradually leveling out until it formed a vast spiked surface, as though 2,000 white-and-red nails had been hammered deep into the face of the city, to form a design for which the guiding blueprint had been lost, or had never existed in the first place. The housing blocks' rigorous system of triangular sequences, legible high above the city, from the base of the Soviet war monument, became scrambled to ocular chaos at ground level, too close to my eyes; as I crossed the Nový Most bridge and passed the facade of the "Europa-Center" shopping complex, the Petrzalka blocks came to form a serrated barrier of pre-cast concrete, seemingly impassable on foot. Even to reach the front line of blocks required a dangerous traversal, with a fast-moving highway of nose-to-tail trucks and cars shuttering the space between the "Europa-Center" and Petrzalka. There appeared to be no other way to cross from the city into Petrzalka or back, and I could see impatient groups of around fifteen or twenty figures on either side of the four-carriageway road, their alert eyes scanning the screaming vehicles coming from both directions, attempting to calculate the exact instant at which they could cross without being flattened; there was no pedestrian crossing, and the evidence of that site's lethal status had been attached to railings alongside the road gutter, in the form of tiny photographs of the dead, most of them elderly, together with plastic flowers, postcards showing precious or revered images, decades-old portraits of Dubček or Stalin, embroidered squares of cloth, and burnt-out candles. I joined the people waiting to cross; the vehicles relentlessly whipped by, and I could understand the sheer contortion of vision necessary to determine the distance between them. From time to time, a few lithe teenagers managed to throw themselves across in split-second intervals, but the less agile looked as though they would be there for hours.

After twenty minutes or so, the traffic from one direction suddenly disappeared completely. There had clearly been a major accident or bottleneck, somewhere along the southern highway, and faced with that mass of bodies in hesitant movement, the drivers on the remaining carriageways reluctantly braked to a halt and let them pass. I entered Petrzalka with them, intending to walk all the way through those lines of towers until I came out on the other side. I found an aperture in the initial screen of housing blocks and began to zigzag my way through them. A wind laced with ice and dust blew between the towers from the plain behind them, and I walked directly into it in order to maintain my sense of direction. Up to the height of six or eight feet, every surface of the housing blocks was saturated with graffiti inscriptions and images, some of them representations of the towers themselves, their minuscule windows and inhabitants' eyes identically rendered as voids, in proficient spraycan gestures; above that height, the facades still held the now-corroded plastic paneling with which they had been encased in the 1970s. At that time, a million or more inhabitants of Bratislava had been uprooted from the city's districts on the other side of the Danube and relocated here, to inhabit a new kind of concentrational city of Europe; they had arrived nowhere, as though participating in an experiment adapted from one of Stalin's great projects of arbitrarily expelling entire populations from one end of the Soviet Union to the other. The inner city of Bratislava had been left near-depopulated, while other districts had simply vanished. I walked for two hours, encountering nobody; the terrain of concrete towers was almost unbroken, studded only with occasional gray-grassed wastelands and emptied-out zones where structural failure had caused a tower to collapse in on itself. Finally, I reached the last line of housing blocks; beyond, the plain stretched out towards the Austrian border.

All through my journey into Petrzalka, I had been looking for traces of the children of those towers, but they were nowhere to be seen. All I had caught were the spraycanned revelations of their lives at the heart of Europe – those images of sex, death, and inflicted power seemingly executed in infinite, harsh leisure, through the night, with occasional excursions onto the overexposed space of the Nový Most bridge walkway. I took a different route back towards that bridge; after an hour, as the dusk began to fall on that city, I arrived unexpectedly at the Petrzalka railway station. Amassed on the concrete plaza in front of the station, and spilling out into the road, the teenaged inhabitants of Petrzalka, hundreds strong, exuded a jagged cacophony, drinking, laughing, and cursing, oblivious to any moment or site beyond those they occupied, at that instant, pinioned on the surface of that burning, spinning planet. I moved between them, across a ground layered with shattered fragments of slivovitz bottles and crushed beer cans, and looked at the station's indicator board; most of the trains carried daily commuters into Bratislava's corporate and industrial districts, to the north of the inner city, but a few international night trains passed only through Petrzalka, eliding Bratislava altogether, as though that city had now been usurped by its urban outgrowth. I left the children of Petrzalka in their uproar and headed back towards the Nový Most bridge, the glowing summit of its elevator tower visible above the lines of housing blocks.

39

I crossed back out of Petrzalka, keeping the summit of the elevator tower fixed in my sight in order to negotiate an oblique route through the slanted sequences of housing blocks. At one point, I found myself poised above Petrzalka, in the emergency lane of a thundering overpass, and had to double back to locate another way through. The dusk had deepened by the time I reached the highway that divided Petrzalka from the Nový Most bridge; the northbound carriageways had reopened, and the vehicles still hurtled by, but their number had diminished by that hour, opening out opportunities for a headlong crossing. Finally, I entered the Nový Most bridge's elevator. The old operator appeared exhausted, leaning back against the rusted aluminum control panel, his polyester suit crumpled under the elevator cage's acetylene striplighting, his mouth inhaling deoxygenated gasps after the long day in that constricted space; but, as I handed him the small coin that paid for my ascent, he smiled in faint recollection and asked politely if I had yet visited the "Europa-Center." I answered no. This time, he chose not to narrate the ascent, leaning back again with his eyes shut, and we rose up in silence; the illumination inside the elevator made the evening city impossible to see, the windows reflecting only the glaringly lit physical contents of the interior, and I looked again at the dense configuration of indentations and channels arranged across the operator's aged face. I mapped that facial network in my mind over the askew, dead-end movements of my journey. Fused together, that encounter of face and journey seemed for an instant to reconcile one another – but the only image that emerged momentarily in my eyes from that encounter was one that flashed and blurred, like a malfunctioning digital screen, veering across time and space, unseizable in its transmutation, half-body, half-city, before extinguishing itself as we reached the summit of the elevator tower.

The operator opened his eyes, stood formally upright and announced the end of our ascent. Then, he shyly added that this was the very last evening on which the café would be open; he and his wife were finally retiring, and the elevator was making its final few ascents and descents, before being closed down. I entered the spherical space of the café, its form designed like a 1970s space-rocket capsule, with a circle of tables evenly arranged around its vast windows; that space revolved above the city, in small jolts, each orbit taking exactly an hour. At the entrance, the operator's wife stood behind a wooden trestle table, like those I had glimpsed inside the ruined mausoleum on the Žižkov Hill in Prague, twenty or thirty identical postcards of the bridge arranged in front of her, its pristine span outlined against the Petrzalka housing blocks at the time of their completion; I bought one and took a seat at a vacant table. At most of the other tables, families were sitting, attentively viewing the city and making observations to one another about familiar sites; the starched pink tablecloths in front of them held glasses of beer luridly colored green and red with chemical dyes. The dusk had shaded almost to nightfall, and the city far below had been irregularly illuminated, the signs blazing on the corporate towers above the inner-city core, the monument on the Slavín hill now darkened, the obelisk appearing only at brief intervals against the sky, its immense black bar imprinted on the rushing flurries of ice clouds.

I took the crumpled map of Europe from my pocket and spread it out on the table in front of me. It had almost disintegrated, and my journey was nearly over. I knew that if, at the last moment, I were still able to locate the image I had searched for, which could embody and project Europe's memory, it would demand a journey to Europe's dead center. I returned to the elevator-operator's wife and bought a souvenir pen, then used it to calculate the midpoint axis between the six cities of my journey: Prague, Budapest, Linz, Kraków, Vienna, and Bratislava. I mistrusted that map as the sole medium by which to make that aberrant calculation, but it formed my only guide. I drew the arms of an X-shape between the four cities at the far perimeters of that journey, excluding the final two cities on the journey's south-central edge. The low-grade ink instantly leaked through the surface of the ragged paper and smeared the tablecloth below. The crossing point of that X-shape appeared to hit the southern suburbs of the city of Brno, a hundred miles or so directly to the north of the Nový Most bridge. I waited until the café's creaking orbit brought me into a northerly alignment, then intently scanned the course of the Danube valley as it headed in that direction; when that river-course began to bend westwards, after a few miles, my eyes still continued on to the north, from elevation to elevation, propelled into a final flying over Europe's cities, attempting to find a way through their darkness.

The indicator board at the Petrzalka station had shown a night train leaving for Brno at three the following morning. I drank the last of my glass of green-dyed beer and walked over to the elevator-operator to ask to be taken back down. It was almost his last descent; only a few hard-drinking café patrons were left, muttering ominously and reluctant to leave, after consuming too much of that chemical-enhanced fluid. The operator punched a well-worn button on the control panel, and we started to sink down to earth; we each said nothing, eyes closed.

40

Before returning to the Petrzalka station to take the night train out of that city, on the final stage of my journey into the urban dead center of Europe, I decided to follow the counsel of the elevator-operator and visit the all-night "Europa-Center" shopping complex: the third and last of the sites he had revealed to me on my first ascent through the Nový Most bridge's tower. It took less than a minute to reach the entrance of the "Europa-Center" once I had descended the concrete stairway that led down from the bridge's western plinth. At ground level, the digital screens that had been vertically tilted into illegibility by my elevator ascent now rectified themselves, impacting directly into my eyes from the roof and facade of the complex, their pixels razor-sharp. I could see from the 1970s photograph on the postcard I had acquired from the operator's wife that, at that time, a vast park of pine trees had bordered the western bank of the Danube; the "Europa-Center" had supplanted that site, its windowless silver oblong now exactly occupying the park's parameters. It was late in the evening, but the car park outside the complex remained filled to capacity, and inside, the place was heaving with human bodies. I understood now why the Petrzalka housing-block terrain had appeared so empty: apart from its oblivious, spraycan-toting children, those inhabitants evidently spent their time either here, or triple-bolted into their plastic-walled, minuscule apartments. I walked through the complex's arcades of marble-clad concessions, each lavishly laid out to caress or grab the eye; the austere fashion-boutiques seemed ill-used, but the alcohol stores were doing roaring business, people pouring out of their exits with liter-bottle armfuls of premium-grade slivovitz. Impelled by that collective action, I bought a bottle too, holding it in my fist until I had reached the far end of those glistening arcades, and had to turn back for the outside world.

Once I had left behind the patrolled zone of the "Europa-Center" car park and crossed the now-deserted highway into Petrzalka, I could feel that the atmosphere had shifted violently from my traversal of that space earlier in the day. I heard distant screams and shouts of fury or pain from every direction. Groups of figures had huddled around fires of debris ignited in the darkened wastelands between the housing towers. All of the streetlights had been extinguished long ago with well-aimed bricks, leaving only the phantom blue glow emitted from hundreds of thousands of television screens to illuminate my way across the Petrzalka terrain. I considered returning to the "Europa-Center" to wait out that night there, but I was already too far into Petrzalka, and began to down the slivovitz in great gulps, to keep calm. From time to time, gangs of fifty or more hooded figures would tear out of the darkness behind me, heading at urgent speed for an assignation somewhere in the night. For the first time on my journey, I began to feel a sense of physical threat, but I knew that with that bottle of slivovitz gripped by its neck in my hand, I had mercifully passed into near-invisibility.

After an hour, I neared the Petrzalka station, approaching it along a pathway that ran beside the railway tracks. The station's plaza was cruelly lit up by its advertising hoardings, and I could see the lines of yelling figures there, heaving and convulsing, as though the entrance to the station needed to be fiercely guarded against some massed assault, though there was nobody attempting to enter. I doubled back along the barbed-wire fencing between the path and the railway tracks, until I found a rip large enough to get through, and walked beside the tracks until I reached the platform from the station's interior side; the noise of the children of Petrzalka still echoed there, the pulses of raw sonic uproar filtering down to banal reverberations as that noise passed through the station building. The empty platform's indicator board showed the night train for Brno arriving imminently. It had already made a great journey, from the Black Sea coast, and was heading all the way up to Europe's northern ports; it would pause at Petrzalka only for an instant, but that was enough for me to vanish from that city.

41

After a few minutes, the train had left the immense blue glow of the Petrzalka satellite city behind, looping around the plain beyond the housing blocks' western perimeter, until it reached the Danube valley; it ran alongside the fast-flowing river for a while, before heading due north into a darkened interzone studded with long-eroded industrial towns. I had finished the residue of indigo-tinted alcohol on the Petrzalka station platform and discarded the empty bottle there; it had served its task of camouflaging me on my walk through that lethal night terrain. But I now made my journey to Europe's dead center in an excruciating slivovitz haze, my head pounding, my eyes painfully registering the factories and stations spinning past the window, just above the level of unconsciousness. The interior of the train was lit by minuscule, bare lightbulbs that made my retinas ache; around me, I heard the sounds of exhausted voices, but could barely make out the reeling faces of the figures occupying the other seats. Only the arrhythmic squealing from the train's wheels and decrepit undercarriage, already pushed beyond endurance by the long journey from Constanţa, kept me marginally lucid for the first hour or so, then I fell into an alcohol-induced blackout. The next moment, an earsplittingly amplified voice was announcing the imminent departure of an express train for Rostock, and I realized I was already in Brno's station, with the train's engine now cranking up to leave that city.

I felt my way to the door and staggered down to the platform as the train heaved into movement. Anyone who also left the train at that station had already disappeared, and the other platforms remained deserted; it was still before five, and even the early-morning commuter trains to the industrial suburbs had not yet started to run. I managed to negotiate the underpass beneath the platforms and emerged into the high-ceilinged, imperial-era waiting hall, illuminated from far above by lines of gilt chandeliers; that entire space pivoted wildly around me. The alcoholic night-inhabitants of the waiting hall were stretched out or seated around a circle of wooden benches, under the station indicator board, some gibbering in subdued fury, others silent, too far gone even to maintain any lament or denunciation. I found a gap between them and prized myself into it. Slumped down, my face in my hands, I could at first remember nothing, of where or who I was, could not identify my body or my eyes from those around me, and remained there, immobilized. After an hour or so, my memory started to come back in glacial bursts: I was supposed to be traveling to the heart of Europe; but, if this were the heart of Europe, then it was simply nowhere. The first passengers now began to traverse the waiting hall, and the station's café opened for its dawn clientele; I stood upright and entered that café, drinking cup after cup of bitter-black coffee until my head cleared.

When it became light outside, I decided to try walking to the station's exit. I looked out: the morning was bright, the melting snow from the final winter storms still on the ground; it was the first day of spring. Encouraged, I took a few precarious steps to the left, past the city's postal building. Turning in the direction of its concrete facade, my eyes still pierced by hangover pain, I came face-to-face with a vast, malfunctioning digital image-screen, the last I would encounter on that journey. Its image quality was low, and the screen had been ineptly screwed to that grimy wall, in danger now of crashing to the ground, the restraining bolts half-adrift at each corner, the power lines and connections trailing off to one side. The images transmitted were in overload, succeeding one another too rapidly, so that it was impossible to determine their corporate allegiance. Finally, they resolved themselves into a freeze-framed image of the earth, its revolving moon a tiny circle behind the planet; within that stalled image, the continents themselves seemed to be frozen, carapaced with an impenetrable layer of ice like that I had seen covering America, at the beginning of that winter, from the window of the Los Angeles-bound airplane. Europe appeared thrown to the edge of the image, that continent half effaced, not at the heart of anything, after all. Looking closely at the image's surface, before its power-source fused completely and the screen turned void, I could only approximate whereabouts in that image I was standing, at that moment, on the city's face, the least fragment of a pixel within that surface.

42

I left that obsolescent image-screen behind, and set out to reach the location in the southern suburbs of Brno where the lines I had inscribed on my map of Europe's heart had formed their intersection. I knew it could well be a random heart whose site I was about to occupy; if the shoddy souvenir pen I had used to pinpoint that X-shaped heart, on my table in the Nový Most bridge's spinning café, had hit the slightest obstruction on that uneven surface, the lines' intersection could easily have occurred somewhere up in the northern suburbs of Brno, or even in another city altogether. But I had located that heart with an unerring, blind gesture; if that heart of Europe had communicated itself to me in some way, to guide my gesture across the paper, as though in some perverse Ouija-board session, it seemed that its forces of mundane banality, oblivious bliss, and imminent violence must have meshed with one another, in a mutant amalgam, for an instant, in order to form that revelation. Holding the overdrawn map in my hand, I now tracked my way through the ankle-deep, melting snow, along the avenue that ran south from the railway station. At the far side of the Svratka river bridge, the avenue abruptly ended, and I had to follow an uphill path that led alongside the course of a tramway. At first, on that ascent, I was getting nowhere, my feet slipping back further in the ice than they advanced at each step, my head still aching from its slivovitz hangover; finally, I reached the crest of the hill, and looked down into the southern suburbs.

I passed the Brno city cemetery and turned into an avenue that sloped towards the vast suburban terrain. In a mid-nineteenth-century tenement building close to that turning, the French writer Jean Genet had once lived for twelve months, as a young man in the mid 1930s, at the end of an immense journey on foot through Europe; beginning on the southern coast of France, where he had deserted from the Foreign Legion, Genet had walked across the entire southern edge of Europe, to Yugoslavia, then up to the cities of central Europe, ricocheting his way between them, engaging in acts of prostitution and theft to survive, constantly arrested and expelled across borders by the police of the countries he traveled through. After he reached Brno in 1936, in a state of exhausted denudation, a refugee organization assigned him into the care of a displaced German-Jewish family; he then lived on the balcony of their apartment in the Dlouhá avenue, sleeping year-round in the open air and descending into the city each day to make a bare living by holding the collecting hat for itinerant street musicians, before suddenly heading off again, still on foot, into Poland and across to Hitler's Berlin, then back to Paris to begin his life of crime. The tenement building had been razed to the ground in the 1970s, its site replaced by one of an intermittent row of tilting concrete-block towers, their substandard facades still more cracked and graffiti-saturated than those of Petrzalka.

A mile or so further down the Dlouhá avenue from the location of Genet's phantom tenement, I came to the point where, as far as I could tell from my now-ruined map of ink-blurred lines, I had positioned the heart of Europe; when I had

117

drawn those lines, the previous evening, on the bridge-tower summit high above the Danube, I had imagined an urban site that would resonate immediately with all of the cities through which my journey had passed, the residues of memory too vivid to be constrained. But the site that my body now occupied badly mismatched the one I had tenuously conceived as the fulfillment of my journey. The intersection point marked on my map coincided on the ground with a suburban tram-stop, on a side road leading off from the Dlouhá avenue; several commuter lines from the outlying suburbs joined together at that tram-stop, and its prominence had been signaled by the erection of an accompanying hypermarket complex. For miles around that site, as far away as I could see, dense clots of slapdash housing towers had been scattered over the hill-sides, interspersed with a few survivors of the now-decrepit nineteenth-century tenement blocks, constructed in that suburb to house the innumerable laborers needed for Brno's then-expanding metal and chemical industries. I stood on the tram-stop's platform and let the time seep by. If I had reached the heart of Europe, then that void site appeared to hold no memory at all, except for the repetitive flashes of involuntary recognition experienced by the commuters who changed trams here, in thrall to the trackside advertising hoardings, caught for an interval in that canceled-out zone, and thinking of sex, or of death, or of nothing at all. It was now late morning, and only a few people were waiting for the arrival of trams into the city. Otherwise, a group of hard-bitten men had congregated at the open hatch of a liquor shack, directly adjacent to the platform, in order to silently down raw vodka and beer; every wooden bench beside the tram-tracks was inhabited by close-packed lines of vociferously disabused children, twelve or thirteen years of age, momentarily liberated from their towers.

43

I stood on the tram-stop platform all through the afternoon, scanning every graffiti'd surface of its concrete shelter, every splintered exterior of the surrounding housing blocks, every facial movement of the surly children and alcoholic men who inhabited that space, searching hard for any trace of memory at that dead center of Europe; but I discovered nothing. At one point, a pounding rainstorm blew out of the east, soaking through my clothes, then the sun came out and the last of the ice gradually melted. Towards the end of the afternoon, floods of people began to arrive back in that suburb on trams from the city's industrial complexes, and the children abruptly left their benches and dispersed, drawn away within the mass of bodies heading for the adjacent hypermarket and the Dlouhá avenue; the men at the alcohol shack stayed put. When the light started to fail, I finally abandoned my ocular search, and boarded a tram with the Brno railway station marked as its destination point. It followed an oblique route, zigzagging for over an hour through the equally void western suburbs, before reaching the inner city, the grandiose sixteenth-century mansions around its central market squares concealed under vast tarpaulins, the buildings' intricately carved facades undergoing a comprehensive corporate overhaul.

Back at the Brno railway station, I passed straight through the waiting hall where I had spent that dawn in incapacitated oblivion, and crossed the underpass to the far side of the station, the overhead rumbling of departing trains penetrating through to that subterranean channel. A sequence of further sub-tunnels fanned out from the end of that underpass, in five branches, each eventually emerging into the open air at petrol-soaked tarmac plazas, where people were crowded around buses leaving for the outlying suburbs. I followed the course of each of those sub-tunnels. All along the sides of the near-dark walkways, the dust-encrusted windows of minuscule stalls displayed every conceivable kind of redundant article for sale: old shoes, tenth-hand magazines, rusted surgical instruments, long-vaporized cosmetic liquids. Peering through the near-opaque windows, I could see the insularized faces of old men and women, sitting hunched on wooden stools in cramped cubicles, seemingly disinterested in the possibility of a transaction, as though such a miracle had last occurred decades, or even lifetimes, ago. A few over-enterprising stallholders had erected trestle tables that jutted out from the walls, laden with detritus and half-blocking the path of the downcast figures rapidly traversing the tunnels; but those figures had become adroit in their maneuvers, and instinctively sidestepped the obstructions.

From the steps at the end of the last sub-tunnel, I emerged up into the evening air beside the lurid facade of a small sex cinema, the "Casanova." It appeared neglected and underused, positioned on the wrong side of the station, away from the main inner-city exit, around which twenty or thirty sex cinemas and multifunction sex clubs did brisk business. I could see hundreds of metal film-cans stacked up in that cinema's foyer, arranged in precarious columns along one entire wall, as though no film ever shown there had been returned to its owners; but I knew that those columns must have been constructed solely for decorative purposes, by the nostalgia- or monotony-impelled staff, since the celluloid reels they had once contained had become long-obsolete and the cinema's films would now be projected digitally. Standing in front of those film-cans, I decided to leave behind the heart of Europe, that night, to rejoin the train on which I had arrived in Brno when it again passed through the station, and this time to remain on it all the way to the Baltic coast, to Rostock, on the far side of the European landmass from the destination of my other escape to the ocean, to Trieste. I entered the foyer and asked the aged proprietor what time the cinema stayed open until. He lifted three wizened fingers into the air, then elaborated, announcing with pride that he showed only Czech films there, the very best quality; those films had been dispatched in ultra-high-definition digital format from the immense sex industries of Prague and Ostrava. I paid the admission fee and entered the overheated cinema of sixty or so worn velvet seats. Most of its rare clientele remained only for a short time, killing gaps between trains, but I had longer to wait for my own northbound express; exhausted from the previous night's journey and the residue of alcohol overconsumption, I slept fitfully in my seat, within the urgent cries of orgasm.

44

At precisely three in the morning, the proprietor began to turn the cinema's lights rapidly on and off to indicate that it was closing time. I had been alone in that space for the past few hours, its other inhabitants sloping away just before midnight for the final commuter trains to Olomouc and Adamov. The film being shown at that moment suddenly snapped off in mid sex act, the arduously grimacing faces vanishing from the screen, the extinguished extra-high-resolution pixels leaving behind a ghost image of human bodies, seared for an instant on my retinas. The cinema's glaring striplighting then remained on, and every last fiber of the stained velvet seats and projectile-damaged screen became over-evident; I made my way back out to the film-canned foyer, where the proprietor shook my hand

and thanked me for my custom, handing me a souvenir book of matches bearing the cinema's name and location, in expectation of a return visit. I put it into the pocket that held my map of the heart of Europe, and headed back through the darkened tunnel to the station underpass, then up the steps to the international departures platform.

The entire station was deserted, every platform empty; only the collisions of wagons being shunted in the marshaling yard to the north occasionally broke the silence. Above the colonnaded station-building, its ornate rooftop surmounted by imperial-era statues of torch-wielding naked women, the aura of light propelled upwards from the inner-city core illuminated the base of low-lying black clouds, traveling west to east at speed. Nearly two hours still remained before my departure, but no trains would stop in Brno in the intervening period, and the platform's indicator board already showed the itinerary of that night express to Rostock, via Prague, Dresden, Berlin; at that moment, it would just be leaving the Petrzalka station, exactly twenty-four hours after I had last taken it.

I reached into my pocket and took out the map of Europe, stretching the wrecked paper in my hands. The map had been soaked through in the afternoon's rainstorm, during my vigil at the suburban tram-stop, and that stretching maneuver was too much for many of its creases. As they ripped, the resulting gaping holes exposed the surface of the platform below; the entire eastern side of the map had turned to pulp. The lines I had inscribed in pencil at the start of my journey, under the dome of the Hlavni Station's old concourse in Prague, linking the cities of central Europe, had now entirely faded away, and I could no longer catch any trace at all of that journey; the names of cities printed on the map, still barely legible the previous evening, at the summit of the bridge café, had been washed away too. The only marks that had survived were those of the X-shape I had drawn across the map in low-grade ink; blurred and jagged, that cross placed over the heart of Europe had somehow endured. I took the book of sex cinema matches from that same pocket and struck three together on its abrasive strip, holding the resulting flame to the underside of that intersection on the map. At first, the rain-saturated paper only smoldered, then the chemicals inside it ignited, and the map flared. At that instant, a non-stop night express entered the station, traveling at high velocity, heading southwest, from Warsaw to Munich, along the track on the opposite side of the platform to that from which the train I was awaiting would depart; the luxurious carriages passed by and I glimpsed the passengers' faces, leaning against the windows, most of them asleep, one or two gazing out, their attention caught for a moment by that minuscule conflagration. Within a few seconds, the train had disappeared; the seething currents that whipped the air behind it suddenly engulfed the glowing remains of my half-consumed map, seizing it from my hands, and it disintegrated in the slipstream, a few brittle ashes hanging in the turbulent air before falling to the center of the track.

As the departure time of the Rostock night express neared, a scattering of passengers joined me on the platform: entire uprooted families accompanied by innumerable sacks of clothing, teenaged soldiers, and a few crumpled businessmen, apparently reluctantly torn from the all-night sex clubs around the station's main exit. Just before the train was due, an old man in a black suit climbed the steps from the underpass, supported by a young woman carrying a battered leather suitcase, and they stood together at the platform's edge. Then the rails began to hiss, and the lights of the night express appeared out of the darkness.

45

The train's carriages were divided into compartments of plastic-coated seating, four places on either side, facing one another. I realized now that the train from the previous night could not have had time to return all the way to Constanţa and then back to Brno; the carriage in which I found an empty compartment came from a more archaic vintage than that of the previous night, its side emblazoned with the Romanian railways' state-industry logo, the corridors lined with prints of the Black Sea coastal resorts. The train moved off and I watched the Brno station recede. The compartment door slid open and the old man entered, the young woman behind him, hauling their suitcase. I stood up to help heave that suitcase onto the wire-netting luggage rack. My face was only inches from that of the old man as he turned towards me, smiling. It was a face still older than that of the Nový Most bridge elevator-operator, nine decades or more of striations cut into the forehead, cheeks and neck. Although I had conceived of the elevator-operator's face as a map, I saw now that it had formed only a preparatory blueprint for my vision of this face, its configuration identical in every respect to the networks of lines I had drawn over the map of Europe that had vanished in flames, an hour earlier. I felt that if I looked deeply enough into that face, I would finally arrive at the heart of the memory of Europe. The face of the young woman, also pressed up close to my own as we levered the suitcase into position, appeared as the exactly inverse surface to that of the old man's face: an unlined, void screen on which memory could never adhere or imprint itself.

I sat down, opposite the old man and the young woman; their faces were held intimately together, and in my exhausted state, those faces' contents appeared occasionally to switch places between one another. The train was circling an escarpment high above the northern suburbs of Brno, before heading through the forests towards Prague. Despite the evident effort it caused him to force words through his brittle voice-box, the old man was eager to talk, either because the ice between us had been broken by my assistance with the suitcase, or simply because, on that night express moving across Europe, it was better not to remain silent; he expelled guttural phrases, bordered by long pauses. After asking the purpose of my own travels, he moistened his lips and began to narrate their journey to Brno. I realized from the first words of his account that the young woman with shorn blond hair, who remained silent, watching the old man solicitously, her lips painted a nonchalant vermilion and her feet encased in army boots, was his great-granddaughter. He had spent some years in Brno many decades ago, and had wanted to see the city again, one final time, though it had changed beyond recognition, and he could barely connect it with his recollections; in any case, he could not have made that journey without the help of his great-granddaughter, who had never seen that city before. Though he said nothing explicitly about his activities during his years in that city, it was clear to me that he had belonged to the German occupying forces, following the invasion of Czechoslovakia in 1939. Now, the two of them were returning home to Berlin, to Lichtenberg, in the eastern districts; his great-granddaughter had accompanied him, since she liked to travel, because, after all, she had been born on the very night on which the Berlin Wall had opened. I asked the young woman how she felt about returning to Berlin. She replied: "It is just a city, like any other in Europe: it is just a city."

Two hours into the journey, after we had talked of the North Sea, the old man drew out a worn leather wallet and took from

125

it a black-and-white photograph of his wife, who had died in the late 1980s, just before the birth of the young woman. I held it in my hand for a moment. In that image, taken in the war years, a beautiful woman of around twenty, with black hair piled above her forehead, wearing a long suit-jacket and knee-length skirt, was sitting on a rock, surrounded by a vast expanse of sand, the sea far away in the distance, behind her; in one corner of the image, a promontory held the buildings of a resort on the northwestern coast of Germany. I handed it back and asked if they had taken photographs during their trip to Brno, but the young woman just smiled, and the old man said that he had intended to, but the shutter of his camera, a Zeiss, faithful for decades, had finally jammed closed shortly before their departure from Berlin. I offered to take a still-image of the two of them together, in that compartment, with the digital camera I had in my bag, and the old man readily agreed, while the young woman pulled a wry face; I could send that image to them, at the first opportunity, by email. It was the only time I had used that camera on my journey. In the viewfinder, I focused on the two faces, the young woman breaking into an incandescent grin, green eyes blazing, the old man grave and intent. I pressed the camera's record button; at that instant, the train's decrepit undercarriage jolted over an obstruction on the track, or a gap between two rails, and my aim tilted violently, the camera sent askew, the two faces fused in a digital blur.

From the moment I took that image, I knew that my journey through the heart of Europe was over, propelled into a definitive free fall of expulsion that would be endless. My eyes' last sighting of Europe was of those two faces, of memory and oblivion, fired together, and my final words in Europe were spoken to those two faces, in parting, as I left that train at Prague's Hlavni Station. Its taillights disappeared north, into the dawn.

Part III

City of Devils, City of Angels

46

I awoke in an anonymous hotel room, with a start, as though I had suffered a strange hallucination, enduring for months on end, or, at the very least, a bad dream. The blinds of the room were closed, the lights were off, and it was impossible at first to determine what city I was in, or the time of day. The humming unit embedded in the wall exhaled the identical air distributed into every hotel room in the world, and the silent television screen flashed the same images that glanced obliviously across the retinas of any inhabitant of any city. I could sense only that I was pitched somewhere high up in the air. I crossed to the window and looked out through the gap between two aluminum slats: with a sensation of horror, I realized that I was in Tokyo. Twenty stories below, I recognized the Shinjuku district's immense terrain of multistory sex-club towers, blazing image-screens, and department-store avenues, propelling their ferocious illumination directly upwards into the night sky. Looking back over the marble-clad concave facade of the hotel, I could see its name marked in great silver letters: "Shinjuku Prince." Straight in front of me, as I faced south, the vast Shinjuku railway station pinioned itself between the infinite blocks of light, extending thirty platforms or more across. From the deserted surfaces of those platforms, I could tell that I must have awakened at around three in the morning: the only point in the day when that station's dense amalgams of fast-moving human bodies momentarily stilled.

The elevator from the hotel's top story slid smoothly down a transparent tube of glass to the foyer; the over-polished floor of that lavish space, its surfaces entirely encased in Swedish granite, reflected the figures of the black-clad night-shift porters. I had been unable to locate my shoes in the hotel room, my wrenched eyes too dislocated to focus, and I walked barefoot onto the still-warm tarmac of the city. The hotel's revolving doorway took me directly to the western edge of the Kabukicho area of sex clubs and bars, the hundreds of neon-inscribed towers ascending seven or eight floors into the air, with further subterranean levels drilled into the ground below the city. In the constricted streets between those towers, scattered clusters of staggering office-workers of both sexes had lost their bearings, too swamped by alcohol to find a way out of the oblique, double-backing alleyways, while a few raincoated girls from the sex clubs strode through at resolute speed, their work over for the night, hair still damp from the exertions of the humid cubicles, their vivid purple-and-white make-up wildly smeared. Groups of apprentice gangsters, their eyes hidden behind sunglasses, scanned every human transit through that area, from their positions in the empty strip of concrete beside the huge Koma cinema-building.

As I passed that building, heading for the Golden Gai area, my memory began to cohere of the split-second blackout I had experienced on the platform of Prague's Hlavni Station, watching the train pull away. Keeping my eyes fixed to the ground, I had then left for the Ruzyně Airport; determined not to speak another word in Europe, nor to register any further image with my eyes, I had bought a ticket from an automatic dispenser for the first available flight. Three hours later, I was in the transfer terminal at Moscow's Sheremetyevo airport, boarding the overnight Aeroflot flight for Tokyo. Once that airplane had crossed the Ural Mountains, I felt the seizure of Europe immediately come apart. Above the Kara Sea, beyond the coastline of Siberia, the Northern Lights appeared, glittering in phosphorescent suspension against the darkness, their presence sealing that miraculous exit. Then the airplane soared over the frozen mountain-ranges and entangled oxbow lakes of Siberia, so identical in appearance to the iced zones of America I had traversed at the beginning of my journey that it seemed as though those zones were being perversely re-created, second by second; after eight hours, the dawn came up and the final spurs of the Khrebet Siknote mountain-range sped away under that airplane's wings. The fissured ochre landmass suddenly ended with a thin spit of white sand, and the luminous Sea of Japan stretched out to the east. The airplane began to hit turbulence over the sheer black peaks of the Japan Alps, and convulsed spasmodically as it descended towards Narita Airport; as it neared the surface of the planet, I fell into another blackout, and my vision snapped-off as abruptly as the image of that planet which I had seen projected from the Brno postal-building's malfunctioning digital screen.

Almost all of Shinjuku's sex structures and bar complexes were less than a decade old, the buildings demolished and reconstructed as soon as they started to show cracks or signs of age; the sole exceptions lined the narrow alleyways of the tiny Golden Gai area, those worn-out two-story buildings constructed in wood soon after most of Tokyo had been incinerated in its 1945 fire-bombing, and now marooned at the far eastern edge of Shinjuku, aberrantly left to stand. I entered the Golden Gai, infinitely far away from Europe. But even expelled from Europe, its images and memories now wiped from my mind, I could still somehow feel myself immersed in Europe and its vanishing.

47

As I emerged from the Golden Gai, the flashing red lights of the huge, fifty-story towers of Nishi-Shinjuku appeared in the distance, their extravagant scale effortlessly crushing down the intervening area of sex complexes and department stores. That crenellated row of municipal buildings and luxury hotels had been constructed out of the delirium of Japan's economic zenith at the beginning of the 1990s; ten or more towers had been arranged in a jagged north–south axis, several of them surmounted by obliquely sheered-away roofs. They formed a dense barrier against the western sky. A sudden sliver of memory, compacting together the Petrzalka housing towers with Hitler's projected mile-high burial-tower, insinuated itself into my gazing eyes, supplanting the Nishi-Shinjuku towers for an instant, but I firmly closed my eyelids to efface that image, then cautiously reopened them. I walked towards those reinstated towers, leaving behind the twisted Kabukicho alleyways and entering the wide, illuminated avenues that crossed Shinjuku, still so empty at that hour that I was able to walk, barefoot, down their center, caught between the department-store facades' relentless image-screens. Halfway across Shinjuku, I passed the railway station, its southern exit still locked, the first of the station staff already on duty, anticipating the two-million-strong torrent of human bodies that would traverse that station's concourse in the next few hours.

I turned off the avenue, into the half-moon-shaped marble plaza at the base of the twin-towered Shinjuku town hall, and looked directly upwards towards its summit, the great convex windows of its top-floor observation decks poised in readiness, high above the city. No one was around apart from the security guards at the entrance to the building. Along the plaza's curved perimeter, at evenly spaced intervals, seven ten-foot-high porphyry globes had been installed, as an excessive gesture, to represent the planet, each of them uniformly dried-blood in color; the raised contours of that planet's continents comprised a shallow layer, just above the level of the surrounding oceans. Japan appeared on those globes as an elongated fragment of detritus which had somehow come adrift from the vast landmass that stretched away westwards towards Europe, that fragment's function apparently being that of forming a useful obstruction able to dissipate the too-raw ferocity of westbound tidal waves, storms, or other calamities, as they attempted to impact destructively upon that landmass; so, in its obstinacy, Japan now had a purpose in the world. I walked from globe to globe, tracing the ludicrously minuscule parameters of Europe on each surface, with my fingertips. Above all, now, I desired a definitive forgetting of Europe, through the imposition of a sheer oblivion that only the headlong frenzy of Tokyo could conceivably provide. But in order to test whether that forgetting had already been permanently sealed shut by my flight over the Ural Mountains, I decided to make a sequence of three journeys over the next days, into the void spaces around Tokyo, where my eyes and body might still remain vulnerable to the memory of Europe.

I left those globes and headed back towards the hotel, to find my shoes, before setting out on the first of those journeys. At the exit of the Shinjuku railway station, the earliest commuters of the day were now beginning to stream at speed through the gates, immediately turning towards the Nishi-Shinjuku towers. I continued along the still-deserted avenue; the dawn was coming up over the Golden Gai, and the department stores' image-screens started to bleach out in the harsh rays of sunlight, their contents now mundane, no longer burning into the darkness. I threaded my way back through the Kabukicho sex terrain, to the north of the railway station, to reach the hotel's entrance; a few orange-clad street-cleaners were busy restoring the alleyways' surfaces to pristine condition, though precious little jetsam had been scattered in any case by the night's alcohol-submerged hordes, and even those who had collapsed in the gutters had done so with discretion.

48

By the time I returned to the Shinjuku station, the southern exit was jammed with human bodies, and I stood to one side, between two pillars, sheltered from the corporeal velocity, for an hour or more, watching the faces of the figures making that harsh traversal into the city. By late morning, the sheer intensity of bodies began to falter, and I entered the station, taking an empty suburban train southwards, down the western side of Tokyo Bay. Through gaps between the passing housing blocks, the ocean became visible at erratic intervals, its surface glistening in the sunlight, the coastline bordered continually by chemical-factory complexes, situated on artificial islands created by landfill deposit. After forty miles of traveling through the infinite suburban tracts, I left the train at Kurihama, and walked inland to that suburb's jetty, where decrepit ferries crossed Tokyo Bay every few hours; on the far side of the bay, ten miles away, the mountainous Chiba Peninsula ran south into the Pacific ocean, from its base in the industrial zones of eastern Tokyo. Every other means of transit across the bay had been closed down, and that ferry now formed the sole route to reach the isolated tip of the scarcely populated peninsula. I joined the scattering of foot-passengers on the open-top deck for the fifty-minute journey; the marine wind, whipping northwards from the mouth of Tokyo Bay, cooled the right side of my face. As soon as the groaning ferry had maneuvered itself away from the jetty and set its course, the pinnacled peak of Mount Nokogiriyama appeared, towering upwards on the far side of the bay.

The ferry collided hard with the quayside at the fishing village of Kanaya, the near-disintegrated wooden stanchions finally bringing its momentum to a halt. A salt-rusted metal ladder was nonchalantly thrown out between the ferry and the quayside, and the passengers cautiously balanced their way across it, the debris-curdled surface of the black seawater 100 feet below. I walked through the village of one-story wooden houses to the cable-car station; apart from a centuries-old track that spiraled up the sheer mountainside, chiseled directly into the rock, that cable-car was the only way to the top. The two old women who operated the cable-car panicked at my arrival; I was the first passenger of the day, and its electricity supply had not yet been switched on. While one old woman heaved down on the enormous electricity lever beside the cable-car, sending sparks dancing all along the metal wire that stretched towards the mountain's summit, the other one ushered me into the archaic red cable-car, and it abruptly set off with a series of splintering sounds. Her worn face was almost as intensively striated as that of the Nový Most bridge elevator-operator, and, like him, she narrated the ascent, but I attempted to eradicate the elevator-operator's face from my mind, and to concentrate instead on the old woman's words: she and her sister had operated the cable-car line ever since it was constructed, in 1962, at a cost of over 200 million yen, as a premium-grade attraction, designed to bring thousands of visitors each year to Mount Nokogiriyama, but now, sadly, almost nobody ever came to that remote site. Looking northwestwards across the bay, as the cable-car approached the concrete shack at its terminus, I could see the vast sprawl of Tokyo, and the forms of the Nishi-Shinjuku towers at its core, supremely negligible from that distance.

From the shack at the cable-car's terminus, there still remained an arduous climb of more than an hour to the mountain's plateau, the pathway occasionally diverting its route through the devil-guarded gateways of minuscule shrines, a few of them still decorated with their original hell-screens, the painted panels depicting the damnation of the souls of the inhabitants of cities. Those hell-screens were the work of the monks who had populated that mountain for many hundreds of years, until they had all been slaughtered in the nineteenth century. The cliff face beneath the pathway had been hammered and polished to a smooth, vertical surface by one entire generation of those monks, across forty or fifty years of grueling and incessant work, in the expectation that the next generation of monks would then sculpt an immense figure of the Buddhist goddess of mercy within that gleaming, flawless surface; but the next generation of monks had turned out to be one of licentious idlers, and no further work had been done on the cliff face. I finally arrived at the plateau on the mountain's summit, from which a sequence of four pinnacles protruded upwards, each of them seventy or eighty feet in height; the ragged, weather-battered trees that covered the rest of the mountain almost reached the top of each pinnacle, but then fell short, ending only a few feet below their sharp tips, and leaving visible an exposed surface of naked blood-red rock. I chose the furthest away of the four pinnacles and scrambled up its side, my feet slipping precariously on the eroded steps that had been scored into the rock, twelve centuries before.

The name of Mount Nokogiriyama indicated the "saw-toothed" or "serrated" pattern of its summit, as viewed at a distance, from the city across the bay, and as I clung to the crumbling surface of that pinnacle, with the glittering ocean spread out far below and the air currents seething around me, images began to rush into my mind, one after the other, of all of the serrated mountains I had seen in Europe, those images unsettling my hard-won sense of oblivion: the peaks of the Austrian Alps that I had glimpsed from the tower above Hitler's Freidberg hill in Linz, and then, once again, the jagged front-line of Petrzalka housing towers that had seemed to bar my way as I tried to cross the road dividing that terrain from the "Europa-Center" shopping complex in Bratislava. But I discovered that I could still expunge those unwelcome revelations of Europe from my mind, just as I had done during the previous night when approaching the towers of Nishi-Shinjuku. As I descended on the cable-car towards Tokyo Bay that evening, the old woman by my side, I knew that I had passed the first of my three tests of Europe's forgetting.

49

On my second morning in Tokyo, I took a subway train from the Shinjuku station to the city's central port, its ferry-terminal building hidden beneath dense networks of looping highway overpasses, alongside the main financial district. To reach Mount Nokogiriyama on the previous day, I had crossed Tokyo Bay at its widest point, where its mouth met the Pacific Ocean; here, at its northern end, the bay narrowed upwards into the channel of the Sumida River, then split through the eastern city. The ferry from the terminal building took only ten minutes to arrive at the quayside of the landfill-created Odaiba Island, on the far side of the bay. During the frenzy of Japan's early-1990s financial excess, that vast flat surface of compacted gravel, originally destined for mundane dockyard facilities, had been transformed into Tokyo's pleasure island, designed exclusively for the city's wealthy young inhabitants, studded with luxurious hotel towers and vast virtual-reality complexes, and bordered by an artificial beach of linen-hued sand. That satellite city's entire contents had been conceived for immediate sensorial consumption; memory was not an asset there, and I felt I would be maximally secure, within that space, from any intrusive resonances of my journey through Europe's heart. Halfway across the bay, the Odaiba-bound ferry fell under the shadow of the Rainbow suspension-bridge, its multiple levels carrying the immense volume of traffic that flowed from the city's core out to Narita Airport; at that moment, directly beneath the bridge's span, two larger passenger ferries passed by, on either side of the Odaiba ferry, both of them on the final stretch of their forty-hour voyages, from opposite ends of Japan: the southern Okinawa island chain, and the northern Hokkaido island. The names of their home ports, Ishigaki and Wakkanai, were emblazoned on their bows, directly below the line of passengers leaning on the deck's rails, eager to disembark after their long voyage, their exhausted eyes scanning the Tokyo bayside skyline.

It was only mid-morning, but the boardwalk above the beach was already crowded with teenaged girls, almost all of them alone, many wearing dazzling silver dresses with pairs of diaphanous angel's wings attached at the level of their shoulder blades, their foreheads and cheeks sprinkled with tiny golden stars, their feet enclosed in black sneakers, and each of them concurring, in their isolation, with Tokyo's momentary fashion imperatives; the sand of the beach below lay untouched by human feet. Clusters of slightly older women entered the marble-encrusted lobbies of the twenty-story hotels arranged along that waterfront, the buildings constructed in undulating arc-shapes so that every window's panorama looked out onto Tokyo Bay. A few teenaged boys headed, furtively eyes-down, from the island's monorail stations into the ultra-high-definition digital arenas and virtual-reality palaces. I ascended an escalator to one of the monorail stations; the train circled above the island's perimeter for a while, then entered its interior, that weed-grown expanse still largely vacant. Most construction projects had been halted for many years by Japan's financial calamities, but a group of theme parks had finally been completed in the very center of the island.

A moving stairway led from the adjacent monorail station, past the theme parks' entrances. To my alarm, the third park along, named "Europe-World," had been constructed to display representations of every prominent or significant site of Europe's cities; the image-screens above the park's gates transmitted vividly pixelated Venetian canals, Andalusian palaces, and Tuscan bell-towers. Though disconcerted by that obstinate re-creation of Europe, after its vanishing, I decided to enter the cavernous warehouse building that held those facsimiles, confident that I could still survive my second test of Europe's oblivion, within that seemingly banal, memory-drained zone. The awestruck young visitors to the theme park adhered to a rigid itinerary in viewing the exhibits, a high-volume commentary speeding them along from site to site. A number of the displays of urban fragments were announced as being of an authentic status, their prestigious contents acquired at high financial cost from the governments or cultural agencies of the countries in which they had originally been located, but the only exhibit that impacted even obliquely from my journey of the previous months was an austere, stone-clad facade from the Habsburg palace complex in Vienna, incorporating the balcony from which Hitler had announced the annexation of Austria in 1938, before an elated crowd. Otherwise, I followed the set itinerary pleasurably, gazing at the decorative details of a wall ostensibly transplanted from a fifteenth-century Bruges merchant's house. Then something abruptly cracked in my perception, and I began involuntarily to visualize a supplanting theme park of Europe's memory, more violently askew in conception even than the Budapest Statue-Park; the "Europe-World" exhibits faded away, to be replaced in my eyes by an engulfing space that displayed the Nibelungenbrücke and Powstańców Bridges, the Noworolski and Oświęcim station cafés, and innumerable Soviet war memorials, all of those sites intersecting with one another, their forms extending infinitely outwards from the surface of Odaiba Island. My forgetting of Europe's heart now half-overturned, I closed my eyes in an attempt to suppress those resurgent sites. Backtracking along the itinerary route, I rapidly exited the theme park's gates and took the first monorail train over the Rainbow Bridge, to head back into the mercifully mind-blurring alleyways of Shinjuku.

50

On my final Tokyo morning, I set out on a journey from the Shinjuku station to the cape that marked the furthest eastern point of Japan, on the Pacific coast. The suburban train crossed the corporate districts and ran along the northern perimeter of Tokyo Bay, before entering the immense industrial zones to the east of the city. After an hour or so, the mountain-range of the Chiba Peninsula appeared to the south, its spine of forested spurs heading downwards, for forty or fifty miles, towards Mount Nokogiriyama and the peninsula's tip. I left the suburban train at its terminus and continued northeastwards on a succession of local, one-carriage trains that stopped at every blighted village within a vast plain where radishes had once been grown, until chemical residues from over-exhaustive cultivation had irretrievably tainted the earth. The few other passengers, all elderly, had their faces shrouded in protective masks and sunglasses. After three hours, a cluster of half-collapsed, redbrick chimneys signaled the edge of that scorched plain, and the train arrived at the isolated brewery town of Choshi; at the far end of the station's platform, I transferred to an ancient tram-carriage that grudgingly covered the final miles to the Pacific coast. The tram-halt closest to Cape Inubozaki was situated within a field of dirt, its metal sign corroded away by sea air; I took a track that threaded through the remains of demolished military buildings, until I saw the cape's elevated lighthouse in the distance, a single telephone terminal at its base, alongside haphazard stalls selling ramen-fast-food and souvenirs. From the cape, beaches of immaculate black sand stretched out far to the north and south, the occasional figures of surfers traversing the beaches or bobbing patiently in the water, waiting for an exceptional wave. A path wound down from the lighthouse to the cape, from which a sequence of islets of seaweed-coated black rock trailed directly eastwards, gradually diminishing in size, until they extinguished themselves within the Pacific Ocean. Due east, many thousands of miles away, but intimately, tectonically close to that cape, the ocean would end at Zuma Beach, above the great urban hallucination of Los Angeles, where my journey had begun.

I took the path down to the cape, then waded out through the ocean, at knee depth, to the obliquely sheared surfaces of the first, then second islets; seven or eight more islets extended on into the ocean, but beyond the one that I had reached, the churning currents between the rocks grew too strong, and I could go no further. I sat on the islet's corrugated surface, within the crashing marine air, and took the digital camera from my bag; I switched it on, then accessed the images I had recorded of those two faces, of the old man and the young woman, in the compartment of the Rostock-bound night express, on the last stage of my journey through Europe's heart. For my third test of Europe's forgetting, I watched the entire sequence, five seconds in duration, on the camera's minuscule screen, then pinpointed and freeze-framed the image in which those figures had been blurred together, at the exact point when the speeding carriage's wheels had suddenly jolted across an obstruction or gap on the track: the face of memory and the face of oblivion intersecting, for that instant. I stared at the image, and let it seep into my eyes.

It began to grow dark and cold, and I had to leave that site in the ocean. I kept the freeze-framed image on the screen, put the camera into my bag and waded back to the cape. At the summit of the path, beside the lighthouse's base, I took out the camera and my notebook, located the page bearing the scrawled email address of the young woman whose face appeared in the image, then connected the camera to the transmission point of the telephone terminal and sent that image to the email address. Once the transmission had been completed, I immediately deleted that image from the screen, to the extent that any embedded image or memory can ever be erased. My shoes leaked seawater, the night fell, and the beacon of the lighthouse above my head came on, its beam sweeping in one direction across the surface of the ocean, then returning in the other direction, momentarily illuminating the sequence of islets at the midpoint of each of those movements; but I felt an eye of Europe closing.